Awake Joy

Early Acclaim

"*Awake Joy* is a lyrical expression of the essence of enlightenment. But do not be deceived by the rare delicacy of the prose. This is a must read of depth and brawn. Every question that the seeker might ask is answered in exquisite detail. Katie Davis leaves no doubt as to what to expect at every turn toward ultimate awakening. Even to the final page, I felt that I was handling pure Essence, perhaps the most beautiful sheaf of pages ever in my rough hands."

~ Mark Waller, PhD, California, *The Dance of the Lion and the Unicorn, Awakening*

"As the world situation becomes more intense, we see the balance as it is expressed in the light of consciousness – also becoming stronger and brighter. Katie Davis is one of those precious lighthouses who beam their joy across the seas of humanity. We are blessed to share her book, *Awake Joy*, with us on our journeys. It is a gift for all seekers of truth and enlightenment."

~ Deva Premal and Miten, Australia, Prabhu Music

"Katie's obvious love of what is real, shines through every page and invites us all to recognize what is ever present."

~ Isaac Shapiro, Australia, *Outbreak of Peace, It Happens by Itself*

"A clear call to wake up to the non-dual Self. In this supremely practical guide to escaping the dominion of the ego, Katie speaks from the heart and avoids the temptation to become lost in intellectual concepts, reminding us of the beauty, joy and timelessness of living in the present moment."

~ Dennis Waite, U.K., *The Book of One, Meet Yourself, Back to the Truth*

"Katie shares with us a fresh vision of the awakened life in honest, elegant language that is a pleasure to read. Her lucid descriptions are accompanied by practical experiments that point you to the direct experience of your true nature here and now. I am happy to recommend her to you."

~ David Dasarath Davidson, N.Y., *Freedom Dreams, Wisdom at Work, Gamble Everything for Love*

"A powerhouse of a book! Katie Davis has captured the uncapturable: a clear view of enlightenment…in plain English. Bravo!"

~ Chris McCombs, WA, *Delicious Silence, Beloved, Lover's Road*

Awake Joy

"Katie Davis has written a spiritual encyclopedia! Everyone interested in enlightenment, spirituality or inner contentment will greatly benefit from this book. Covering every topic from the inner workings of the mind, Advaita, meditation and awakening, Katie leaves no stone unturned, no experience uncovered. A great celebration and teaching from one who is obviously Awake and living Joy."
~ Kip Mazuy, Australia, Bliss Music

"To be human is a profound choice. We can direct our attention to the evening news, the Resurrection, or past lives, chakras, heaven and hell, the World Series, or, as right now, to a line of text. Or we can allow it to shift from these endless specifics to the clear space of consciousness within which all this moves and rests. Here the conflict of competing theologies is laid to rest. Katie Davis apparently has some intimate knowledge of this mysteriously simple truth-place and her book will send you spinning round it like a moth round a flame. With luck, or grace, or utter abandon, you may even fall into the flame. If there is a path to peace now, when armies of competing faith face off, it is in this simple, primal teaching. Onward."
~ Michael Green, Pennsylvania, *The Illuminate Rumi* Books

"In this luminous book, Katie Davis reminds us again and again that we are all the very essence of *Awake Joy,* 'a sacredly peaceful joy, which lies deep in every being.' Katie allows us to further understand the nature of the awakening process and the exquisite liberation and joy of a life lived in timeless presence. This is a book whose invitation on every page is to discover the deepest Truth of who you are, beyond the personal self and the story. It is beautifully written by Being Itself."
~ Victoria Ritchie, Spiritual Counselor, Manager of the California Institute of Integral Studies
Editor of *Practicing the Power of NOW*

"*Awake Joy* is a wonderful guide to our awakening, describing the process of conditioned tendencies that dissolve into conscious awareness of our true nature. It is well written with a nice poetic flow. This book explores every conceivable angle of "me" returning home. Through Katie Davis' open invitation to stay in the Now, this could be an easily available resource and a place to turn, when you recognize your avoidance of Now."
~ Fred Campbell, Washington, Eastside Satsang and A Course in Miracles Facilitator

Awake Joy

You are Life's purpose *the Heart of the universe*

~ Katie Davis

Awake Joy

The Essence of Enlightenment

Katie Davis

Awake Spirit Publishing
Hawaii, USA

Awake Spirit Publishing, #202
1993 S. Kihei Road, Suite 21
Kihei, HI 96753 USA
www.AwakeSpiritPublishing.com

ISBN: 978-0-9800912-2-9

First printing, January 2008 in the United States

Printed in the United States of America

Book and Cover Design by 1106 Design

Publisher's Cataloging-in-Publication data

Davis, Katie
    Awake joy : the essence of enlightenment / Katie Davis.
    p. cm.
    ISBN 978-0-9800912-2-9
I. Spiritual life 2. Self-actualization (Psychology). 3. Change (Psychology).
4. Consciousness. 6. Self-perception. 7. Self-evaluation. I. Title

BL624 .D3175 2008

291.4421—dc22   2007940665

Table of Contents

Gratitude

Eckhart Tolle, I am grateful for your encouragement to write this book. It is through this inspiration that *Awake Joy* has taken form.

Victoria Ritchie, Kirtana and Fred Campbell, I thank you for your critique of the initial manuscript. As well, Sundance Burke, Deva Premal and Miten, Isaac Shapiro, Dennis Waite, David Dasarath Davidson, Dr. Mark Waller, Chris McCombs, Kip Mazuy, Michael Green, Barbara McDowell, Gangaji and Eckhart Tolle, I appreciate your early reading and sharing.

I am grateful to those who supported my departure to write this book and to those whose efforts have supported this teaching in so many ways. I would especially like to thank Susane Matlock for her wonderful organizational skills, as well as Fred Campbell for his energetic event coordination.

Mark and Sheri Bocci, I appreciate your friendships, welcoming and kindness, as well as other friends, colleagues, volunteers and organizers for your help, presence and for simply being who you are.

I love you Jodie, Summer, Shannon, Ryan, Kaileen, Cadence, Brayden, our families, as well as my best friend passed at only age ten, Sherry Whinnery.

In closing, words cannot express my gratitude to my husband, Sundance Burke. We have journeyed this adventure for twenty years and I feel so fortunate. I am not sure if there are many, who could have written two books at the same time, with their desks side by side. Beloved, I cherish every moment.

Introduction

Book Origin

More than twenty years ago, I awakened spontaneously without spiritual practices or teachers. I briefly share the awakening story in Chapter Two of Part IV: The Heart. Twelve years later, I met Eckhart Tolle, the author of the internationally acclaimed bestseller, *The Power of Now*. I was invited to assist on tour and in the beginning, worked in his offices. Subsequently, I began traveling to share my realized truth; offering the message of true freedom and joy. Over the years, I was fortunate to occasionally visit with Eckhart and he would gently pose, "So Katie, are you writing?" It is through Eckhart's encouragement that *Awake Joy* has taken form.

Meditative Reading

The purpose of this book is not to teach you, since I cannot provide who you already are. I am dedicated to the joy that is consciously emerging within you. I am not here to dismantle the mind's beliefs. I am here to welcome you to discover what lies beneath. If you are willing to harmonize and embrace that which is beyond conscious beckoning and if you are willing to investigate, all suffering dissolves into passionate joy and reappears as true you. This book is a messenger to share that there is a simple and pragmatic way out of suffering into changeless joy.

I would like to offer a few pointers about how to benefit most from this book. *Awake Joy* is suitable for meditative reading, which means that the words resonate with a deeper consciousness that is already within you. Instead of mindfully reading, approach this book in the same manner that you would a meditation. To be more present and open to the inner resonance, I recommend that you enjoy a short exercise before you begin each sitting. It might also be a useful tool for periods of inquietude or struggle. People have shared that it is equally helpful to open to a greater potential of creativity such as before writing, painting or composing. The goal-oriented, mind-made self would rather have you get started and get on with the reading. That is what the ego does; always in a hurry, it rushes to the future. This is not about the future and it is not about the mind. It is about how to get over the superficial mind in the recognition of what is truly here. For convenient access, the exercise is in Appendix I "Preparation for Meditative Reading" at the end of this book.

Meditative reading does not really require a reader and it is not necessary to mentally read for content. Instead, *be* the reading and disappear into it by simply resting in silent being. Read slowly, so that you are aware of the words emerging from the silence and then follow them back into the silence. Notice that as your eyes move, you are still. While reading, please recognize that language and thought are dual in nature, meaning that they always express "two." There is a "subject" that acts by the means of a verb, upon an "object" of every sentence. Enlightenment transcends this subject-object relationship. It focuses on the non-dual or "not two." For this reason, this writing may seem to have paradoxes, which are contradictions. Dual language is sometimes inadequate to express that which is non-dual and unified. This may sometimes give the appearance of inconsistencies.

The current in which the words appear is more important than what the words are saying. "What the words are saying" is symbolic and conceptual. The Heart is beyond the conceptual mind and therefore, it cannot be conceived by ideas. Meditative reading is concerned with how the words resonate deep within you. It is not *what* made you feel the impact of the words. As the sage Jean Klein once said, "it is the *feeling* of the impact." This feeling is called "resonance" and it is a feeling of openness and peace. This requires inner attention as you read. Focus on the *feeling* rather than the *understanding*. This feeling is prior to thought. You observe the "inner-standing," instead of the understanding, as the rare born mystic, Sunyata, once shared. The words on this page are arising within you, so just let them pass into the silence of the Heart, without mental consternation. You cannot look outside yourself for meaning, for the knowing is inside. As you move beyond the world of experience for awakening, you are moving beyond concepts. Self-realization is *being That*, rather than *about That*. After you have completed a reading session, be aware of the mind's tendency to conceptualize the words or possess them. Instead, simply be done. Now, your extraordinary teacher is the inner impact of daily life. With inner attention, always remain open to feeling a deeper resonation.

If you have questions about the reading, please recognize that this is mind activity. Just let them pass as you did while reading the sentences in the book. Follow them back to the silence. Let them rest and inquire inside. If you feel reaction or identification with a concept, these are the activities of desire and fear. Perhaps they are pointers toward something unconscious within you that, when exposed, will reveal that you are free. Please remember that without inquiry, rejection or acceptance is the same mistake. I am not asking for either disagreement or agreement. I am requesting investigation. Investigation does not mean to intellectually process, evaluate or philosophize. Instead, simply be aware and present, with whatever is within you.

The Book Title

Awake Joy symbolizes the Heart; the source from which the universe flows. This manifestation is inseparable from the Heart's power, yet the Heart is not affected by the appearance of form, nor its disappearance. The Heart is the essence of everything that is and therefore directly experienced by everyone. Nonetheless, most are not yet consciously aware of it. Permanent and conscious awareness that you are the Heart is known as Self-discovery or Self-realization.

The Essence of Enlightenment is uninterrupted Self-aware Being, rather than the awareness of being, which remains dual in its expression and realization. Whereas, non-duality stands free of all subjects and objects; there are not two.

The Heart is "awake" or conscious. It is an alive, supreme intelligence that is purely being. Heart is synonymous with "joy" or bliss. It is a living "joy" that is "awake." While the "essence" of enlightenment is quintessentially indescribable, its nature is being-consciousness-bliss, or simply unbroken and enduring *Awake Joy*. While these words may appear to be separate attributes, they are consistent and indivisible throughout the unified field. The purpose of this book is to be a signpost toward the recognition of this field within you.

Terminology, Structure and Format

Whenever I apply such words as Heart, Essence, Reality, Unknown, Self, Life, Awareness, or Truth, among many others, I am pointing to *Awake Joy*. The first letter of the word will be highlighted by capitalization. When I refer to the Self, I am not speaking of the individual self. The Self is the Essence, whereas the individual self is the ego, the idea of "me." The Self is impersonal, prior to individuation and free of any facet of the personal.

Frequently, the terminology of this book may not correlate with traditional English definitions and sometimes may not even be found in the dictionary. The expressions were contrived to describe the truly inexpressible, but directly realized. Nothing in this book has been derived through theory, philosophy, psychology or concept. Likewise, I invite you to discover true Source, through your direct investigation in lieu of conceptual learning. Do not crystallize an observation into a concept, but rather remain open to deepening.

I would like to emphasize that I am aware that some of the terminology in this book may have different connotations in other teachings, religions or philosophies. These terminologies were creatively assigned at the time of discovery. Having never heard of awakening, I created a somewhat new vocabulary as well as new definitions for old words. For this reason, comparison of terminology with other teachings is futile, whereas your feeling resonance is essential.

The structure of *Awake Joy* encourages conscious awakening. It invites your participation in order to unveil the Heart of Life and points to conscious full embodiment. The format is as follows. Part I: "The Dream" presents an overview and an awakened perspective on the world of form and experience. Part II: "The Eyewitness" is an exploration of form in dual consciousness. It points toward direct inquiry and participation, rather than conceptual learning. The chapters shift the reader's attention from "outer" object consciousness, meaning external people and world circumstance, toward the "inner" space of the reader. Finally, it contains several pointers to facilitate the realization of present wakefulness. Part III: "The Pure Being" begins the crux of enlightenment that follows through to the end of the book. It points toward detachment from form and all that is "not Self." The chapters reflect the various integral steps to realize one's true identity. It also focuses on common remaining delusions. Part IV: "The Heart" draws the Self-realized reader from the depth of Pure "I," toward the discovery of That which is everywhere. It encourages a healthy return to non-dual, harmonious living. In Appendix I, I offer a "Preparation for Meditative Reading" to be enjoyed before each reading and Appendix II presents "Practices and Meditations" that help reveal simple being through direct experience. The "Index of Quotes and Lyrics" is an alphabetical listing by teacher, author or artist that appears in this book. Finally, I provide my contact information and a listing of my websites.

The rose symbol is used when I recommend that you pause to directly investigate. This handbook can be your loving friend, loyal companion and gentle reminder throughout your journey, if you are willing to first read and then investigate. It can be reread periodically and it will be fresh and ever new. Initially, if you choose to read this book from cover to cover, I suggest that you then reread the beginning sections in order to clarify where you are in the awakening process. You will then have at hand the unique pointers for deeper realization. Subsequently, put your handbook aside once again for investigation of those pointers. Each time, read only as far as you have clarity. Stop when you notice any attempt to abstractly understand. In this manner, *Awake Joy* will gradually point the way to Self-discovery and the full embodiment of the Heart.

PART 1

The Dream

"Could there be more to this life we call 'mine'
Than a journey through space or storyline? –
More to life than the body can sense
Than the mind can conclude from experience
Does who we are begin with breath,
Depend on form or end with death? –
Strip away these roles, these names
And tell me what remains
And who you really are, who you really are"

who you really are
From the CD "this embrace" by kirtana

Chapter One

The Joy of Being

"I have one drop of knowing in my soul.
Let it dissolve in your Ocean."
~ Jelaluddin Rumi as translated by Coleman Barks

Near a bamboo forest, a lovely Monarch butterfly silently dances through the stillness of tropical Koa trees. As it flutters its path, it hesitates momentarily in midair, as though suspended in space by an imperceptible sacredness. Its graceful wings flaunt deep hues of sunset-orange and are distinctively dappled with tiny full moons of translucent white. As though in chase, a native approaches. He pauses to greet me in the spirit of love and welcoming, so delightfully traditional of island life.

"I see that you have a net." I query, "Are you hunting?"

The butterfly fans its willowy wings, while poised on a crown flower, just behind the man's left shoulder. The local replies, "I have been searching to net a Monarch butterfly. In the islands, it is believed that if we capture a Monarch and then release it, we will be graced with bliss and joy throughout all time."

"May I invite you to stop your hunt, if only for a moment, to sit with me in the silent beauty of this grove?" As he settles across from me with an inquisitive gaze I share, "Truthfully, joy has no cause. It awaits you right here. *You* are the only answer."

He diplomatically refutes, "I am a 'child of the island.' I know that only a Monarch has the sanctity to bless everlasting bliss and joy. This promise has been passed down through the generations, ever since the Monarch was brought to our island from India."

"You can believe what you have learned in the past or you can investigate the truth right now. It takes no time, because joy *is* here. In fact, bliss and joy are always here, since they are within you. Go ahead and inquire. What is here right now?"

In receptivity, he intuitively closes his eyes to silently pose the question, as he focuses intensely on the here and now. Suddenly, he is overwhelmed by a glimpse of ineffable love, sacred peace and the sweet bliss of joy. Gradually, he is consumed by laughter and tears stream his face, as he reflects on his arduous hunt and the futility of his lifetime search for happiness. He had searched everywhere, but *here*.

We continue to sit silently in the frequency of being and then he finally asks, "Why do I feel so happy?"

"This is the Heart of Life and I call it *Awake Joy*. It is the Truth of who you really are."

Grateful for freedom, the graceful Monarch takes flight.

Chapter Two

Open to the Unknown

"Beyond the beauty of external forms, there is more here: something that cannot be named, something ineffable, some deep, inner, holy essence. Whenever and wherever there is beauty, this inner essence shines through somehow. It only reveals itself to you when you are present."

~ Eckhart Tolle

Truth and Relative Truth

Just as in the tropical grove, you have the capability to realize the joy of true fulfillment. You simply open to the inner Unknown. It requires that you remain alert and stop searching. I am pointing toward a sacredly peaceful joy that lies deep within every being. It exists without condition or need and its simplicity is incomprehensible to the mind. Joy's subtlety is imperceptible to the senses. Yet, since it is your Essence, you can realize this Field of Forever Now. Within you, there is an undifferentiated intelligence that contains infinite potentiality and creativity. It is numinous, unconditionally loving, steadfast and absolutely indestructible. Upon revelation of this unfathomable dimension, joy consciously outpours and its realization is life's purpose.

The parable of the Monarch speaks of the Truth of being. This Truth is not a conceptual truth. That is, it is beyond that which could be taught or learned. It is not relative, meaning it is beyond truth and falsehood. It has no opposition and therefore, it is beyond knowledge and ignorance. Absolute Truth is not a philosophy or theory, both of which involve the normal functioning of the dual mind. It does not require a leap in faith and is readily accessible for your direct realization. This Essence is your innermost being that is untainted by conditioned existence and it is your natural oneness with life.

The End of Suffering

To recognize that which is beyond the mind, it requires stillness of thought. However, Essence does not depend upon the quiet mind. Whether there is movement of thought or no thought, Essence is ever-present. It is the undivided eternal life, prior to the animation of all form. It exists before its differentiation into form, such as a human being, or any other being, such as a lovely flower or a beautiful tree. It is the formless fabric upon which the patterns of form appear and the Life that supports all life. The realization that you are this indescribable Essence consumes everything personal in its recognition. Yet, you remain the Essence of the joy of being within the Heart of all beings. The realization of Essence is the end of the delusion of unawareness and this Self-discovery is called enlightenment.

The luminosity of this revelation is so extreme that it destroys the illusion of suffering. You are freed from the concept of time and the false image of "me." Instead of being obsessed with the self-image and its problematic life story, you innately turn to see what the image is representing. You are the true representation and you are so radiantly beautiful! This is not a physical beauty, a personality attribute or a result of a certain behavior. You are unimaginable. The wonderment of your beauty is sublime and without qualification. You are the very Essence of *Awake Joy*. You may be amazed to discover that the assumed identification with the mental construct named "me" is the actual source of your suffering. Its reflection in the world of form is the misery of humanity. The living answer to this misery lies within you.

The Diamond

If I were to tell you that you could possess a million dollar, multi-faceted diamond buried in the ground beneath you, more likely than not, you would start digging. Even though you would not directly know whether the diamond truly existed you would investigate, because you could perceive its value. Yet, when I speak of the diamond of incomprehensible joy and abundance that awaits your discovery, few actually hear this call and earnestly look within. Instead, in disbelief, the "normal" conditioned human being often dismisses this opportunity. They continue what they believe to be a more rational search within the life situation in the hope that the future will provide, what the past has not. True fulfillment does not exist within the confines of time. It is here now, free of the imagined past and future. Fulfillment emerges into the life situation, upon the realization of Essence. Others might have already given up the search for true happiness to endure mediocrity. They might dismiss this invitation in the belief that everlasting joy does not exist.

The objects of the search for happiness within form obviously differ from person to person. People sample many different things, while yearning for fulfillment. Their search may include such mediums as achievement, possessions, career or relationships. This objective search may indeed provide a fleeting, relative happiness. By relative, I mean a happiness that comes and goes. It changes and is therefore impermanent. Relative happiness is in relationship with sadness. It is defined by the lack of sadness. Conversely, sadness is defined by the lack of happiness. Indeed, there are many degrees along the continuum between them. They are opposites that depend upon one another for their definitive existence. They are mutually exclusive and only time separates them. Trapped within the cycle, you are in constant vacillation. One could say that it is through sadness, that you know happiness. In other words, you cannot be happy, without the fluctuating experience of sadness. To the contrary, *Awake Joy* has no opposite. It is transcendent of the happy-sad continuum. Essence is deeper and preeminent. It is free of the cycle, just like you.

The realization of this freedom requires dismissing the known. If ever-present joy is not presently *known* to you, it is obvious that your mind must be open to the *unknown*. The unknown is free of assumptions, beliefs and concepts. It is free of a known past, as well as free of a projected future that is always based on past experience. To inquire into the unknown, it requires your direct investigation. *Awake Joy* cannot be realized without looking, just like the million dollar diamond could not be found without digging. However, I am not asking you to start searching. I am asking you to stop searching and gaze at the diamond that is already deep within you.

As conditioned humans, we seek adventure in becoming. Yet, because this compulsive search is ultimately unsatisfying, we then seek refuge in the peace of being. Once we realize both the complexity of becoming and the simplicity of being, *Awake Joy* emerges. Its Essence is the rapture of true fulfillment. It is a mystery that the human being fears the Unknown, when our love for it birthed us into existence.

Chapter Three

The Secret Ocean

> *"Happiness is causeless. You think that it has a cause —*
> *a lovely car, a beautiful woman, a lot of money, a nice*
> *house, a prestigious job. But when you look deeply,*
> *you will find that when you are actually in happiness,*
> *there is just happiness with nobody who is happy and*
> *no cause of the happiness. This is your real nature."*
>
> ~ Jean Klein

Seashells for Happiness

The Oregon Coast is beautifully lined with lush evergreens and rugged cliffs. The morning fog is mysteriously receding like the *Mists of Avalon*, while the smoke from our cabin's chimney is inviting a cozy, fireside breakfast. I hear a cry from a lone seagull soaring high in the sky and when I look up, I appreciate a bird's eye view of the ocean, sand dunes and old growth forest. The children are beachcombing for seashells. Summer finds a sand dollar and as she repeats its legend, I can see that the story has passed to another generation. We contemplate the intricacies of the five-petal Easter lily on the shell. In tradition, she is about to crack it open to release the five white doves from within to spread

9

goodwill and peace. Instead, she notices the spines on the shell and realizes that it is still living. Jodie then approaches with her seashell pail and we sit together in the driftwood to listen to the sound of the ocean within each shell. Suddenly, forgetting their seashells, the girls scurry off to find other treasures.

In a way, life is like beachcombing, as we search for seashells to find happiness. Seeking love, we carefully gather the treasures that we cherish most and when the happiness wanes, we move on to collect others. We seem to forget that their abundant Source is the Ocean; the only spring of true happiness.

Love surrounds us and it originates from the Ocean within you. We do not need to seek love for living, in the same manner that the spinner dolphin does not cry for water while swimming. The mind has its idea of perfection and what it needs to be happy. All the while, we are the very joy that we are seeking. The separate self is the time-based mind's attempt to divide and it will prove to be futile, since separation is unattainable. Its sense of lack is its own demise. Whereas Self-realization is an ease, since it is already complete. Fulfillment means completion, not a fractional part and love's completion is the discovery of who you really are. After all, a drop of water does not separate to be a part of the ocean, but rather dissolves its partiality.

Desire inherently contains its opposite, which is fear. So while we are creating our personal desires, we are also creating poverty, greed, sexual obsession, power over others in the herd and every form of lack. In other words, when we desire, we are also saying that we lack. Consequently, both seem to be created. If we are acquiring in order to be happier at a future time, ever-present joy will elude us, since it is not a future endeavor. It is here now, uncaused and free of every-thing. The dual mind will prove to be ravenous for its desires, as it runs from its fears. Its bottom line will always be "more!" When it finally discovers that its treasures only provide a fleeting happiness, it discovers the root of its longing; the realization of the Heart.

Before awakening, I discovered what I thought was the mind's ability to create in the seventies. I taught my students and later my children this miracle of creation and they attained their goals as well. Yet, the things and attainments simply came and went. In the end, something always seemed to be missing, so there was always something more to create. I did not realize that the something missing was innate in my uninvestigated assumption of being a fraction of Totality; a separate self wandering through life for meaning. Eventually, only "I" remained and its assumption of separation was its lack and longing. In the miracle of mind-creating, I thought that I was the finger pointing to the moon, the creation. In fact, I was neither finger, nor moon. In retrospect, *observing* was the power. It revealed thought's mechanisms and its images for a deeper self-understanding. Ultimately, only the overwhelming fulfillment of joy sustained. The Heart is ceaselessly outpouring love. Are you looking from the Heart or from the mind?

The space around "I" is joy's way. You are welcome to continue collecting things to try to fill that space, as some sort of future compensation, but things and circumstances within time is not where joy resides. In the meantime, you needlessly suffer, while hoping for personal empowerment that at best can only be partial. Sooner or later, it will be recognized that the space around all of your accumulations is the direction and that it originates within. Essence is deeper than "you and your thoughts" and more profound than "your attention." It is the pure attention of the loving Heart; the only omnipotent power of the universe: Love.

So now, or later, it does not really matter, as long as you do not mind suffering and world hostility. I understand that you may still choose to cruise in a yacht on the surface of the ocean and remain oblivious to the charm of an undersea world that is brilliantly colored with tropical fish. However, the silence of the ocean's depth would be overlooked. You would not become acquainted with the beauty of the coral reefs and the underwater song of the humpback whales, whining in the distance. You also have the option of diving in to explore the unfathomable depth of the inner Ocean. Yachts are fun, but that fun fades and becomes no more than a past mental image. It pales in the joy of your ineffable beauty.

Wisdom's invitation is to dissolve like a sugar cube in a hot cup of tea. You may fear that "sugar" will no longer exist. Nonetheless, take your first sip and see that sweetness remains. If you have realized that now is the only possible time in the universe, then as Rumi so poetically wrote, "Don't wait any longer. Dive in the Ocean. Leave and let the sea be you." The Ocean is the calling and it is your passionate magnificence!

Chapter Four

The Garden of Splendor

> *"Why are you unhappy? Because 99.9% of everything you do and everything you say is for yourself ... and there isn't one."*
> ~ Wei Wu Wei

Fall from the Garden

Innocently enough, a most significant falsehood is passed through the generations. The effect of this original delusion has an enormous impact on a lifetime. The basic flaw is our belief in the image of "me," our concept of limitation to our body and our idea of separation. I refer to this tri-fold assumption as the fall from the Garden. Our parents taught us a hypothesis and we unequivocally accepted it. We identified with a false image and we fell into an abstract illusion that separated us from the Heart, through concept alone. When we identified with the idea of "me," we aligned with nothing more than a mental construct. Just like our parents, none of us investigated the presumption to discover the truth. Instead, the premise was assumed. My mother once shared with me that when I was very tiny, I used to frequently ask, "When did I become a girl?" Perhaps, I was sensing the Garden of Splendor and then became confused, when I became a concept.

As soon as the false assumption of "me" was conditioned, we began identifying with an empty idea of who we are. However, if you are willing to investigate Now, you will find that this idea of separation has no basis and that the image is not pointing to the finite body. On the other hand, if you continue to believe in the false assumption, you will tend to live mentally, experiencing only a fraction of the greater life. Please do not ponder the relative truth of what I am suggesting, since pondering is abstract. To discover fact, inquire within and observe. Without inquiry, a new concept would remain philosophical theory as well. In other words, the conceptual acceptance of what I have found to be true, without your investigation, is equal to the primary assumption. You would be adding more theoretical knowledge to the basket that you empty in order to discover your true identity. I am advising that you scientifically observe what really is within you. The invitation is to investigate "I" to its core. In the process, layer after conditioned layer is shed to discover your Essence.

The Dream of Form

In the "original separation," you were taught to point to the body, when you said "I." This supposition was believed without scrutiny. In theory, this concept assumes that a massive field of conscious intelligence that is referred to as Totality, can be limited, confined, separated and housed in an individual form. This is more ludicrous than trying to pour all of the world's oceans into a tiny teacup. Totality is simply total and cannot be separated. It includes the body appearance, but cannot be limited to form alone. The effect of believing in the original separation is that you identify with the body that has a conditioned intelligence that is less creative and it casts a shadowed veil of separation onto life. Conceptual living is similar to imagining that you live in darkness, even though you are actually living in the full light of day. In darkness, you do not have clear sight. However, if you will investigate, you will find that in the light of consciousness, darkness cannot prevail. It is true that your investigation begins within the body, which is the portal to Essence. However, it is only an entry point. The body is then honorably surrendered as not your true identity. To discover the core of true Essence, attention shifts deeper within the body and then beyond. As long as you believe that your *identity* lies in your individuality and that this identity is limited to your body, the conscious realization of fulfillment is not an option.

By believing in the concept, "I am the body," you are unconsciously living the dream of form. The dream is based on separation, which results in desire and fear. It creates an unquenchable appetite for attainment, achievement, acquisition and becoming to camouflage the ego's sense of lack, which is caused by the blind acceptance of its primary delusion. Above all, it creates more opportunities for you to suffer. You experience anxiety, tension, worry, want, need and stress. Since desire and fear walk hand in hand, the dream also creates fear that is embodied as competition, depression, anger, pseudo power, alienation, resentment and hostility. The ego fears psychological annihilation and unconsciously equates it with the death of the body. It's most primal fear is lack of existence, embodied as a deep desire for survival. Since most of humanity still lives within the confines of body consciousness, some believe that they are marching toward their inevitable death into potential non-existence. This creates a vast darkness in the collective consciousness as we share humanity's vulnerability in form and the delusion of our limitation.

The fears are then projected onto the mirror of life and you witness in the world your concepts that are based on your deepest fears. Humanity has been evolving through this pain and suffering for eons. In the dream world, you observe the hostility of wars, the rage of violence, power struggles, greed, obsessions, alienation and every form of lack, including survival needs, such as food and shelter. That points to insanity. What is this distorted mirror of life pointing toward within you? The resolution is inquiry and your revelation of all that is false and unconscious.

Are You the Conditioned Child?

A newborn has perfect vision at birth, until its eyes are treated for potential disease from its mother. From this treatment, the baby is blinded and the moment of clear-seeing with parents is lost to state-mandated fear. The opportunity to gaze past one another's eyes into the Heart of the soul is missed. Parent and child lose the intimacy of one soul seeing. Lost to this fear is the gift that a newborn offers the forgetfulness of its parents. The newborn's gaze communicates absolute wholeness that is innocent and pure, totally free of forgetfulness.

A minister once shared a true story with me that I would like to share with you. She told of a family with a troubled six year old, whose mother gave birth to his sibling. At home, the family carefully watched the problematic older child, to keep him away from the newborn. They were afraid that the rambunctious child might harm the baby. While the baby was sleeping one evening, the family suddenly noticed that their older child was no longer in the living room with them. In fear, the mother hurried to the nursery. When she opened the door, she saw her six year old holding onto the outside bars of the crib. He was peering through the bars into the wide open eyes of the infant. The mother was just about to reprimand her son, when she heard him speak to his newborn brother, "Could you tell me who God is? I am already starting to forget."

A newborn does not experience that it is separate from its mother and its environment. The baby is not capable of objectifying its parents and the world. Its gaze is expansive and it is not conscious that it has a body. Free of the duality of thought, the baby is innocently whole and free of limitation to form. As conditioning begins, the child is taught that it can be physically separated from its mother. Then, the baby is surprised and fascinated, when it sees its own hand for the first time as it develops body consciousness. The growing child then learns to point to the body as its personal reference point. It begins to assume an individual sense of self, which is confined to its form. The reference point is that of a subject, which perceives other separate objects in the world. By equating and limiting to body consciousness, the child has already objectified itself from its true Essence. The conceptual separation causes an alienating split, as the child experiences itself as another worldly object. The innocent unity and harmony of being the Heart of God is concealed by inherited assumptions. With wholeness seemingly lost, a lifetime of lack begins as fear creeps in unnoticed, with the help of well-meaning parents. The child's fate is a lifetime of longing for a return to wholeness, a return to the Garden of Splendor. If one teaches prayer, the child learns to pray to a separate God that is reduced to a mental concept that requires a leap in faith. This is a leap that some may not make. The wonder of wholeness becomes the imagined reality of being alone. Separated from the Truth of being by notion, the parents then teach gentle kindness and basic goodness from a dual point of view. These qualities are foreign to every ego. Nonetheless, deep within the core of the child, the Heart remains lovingly open.

Freedom Child and Conscious Parenting

The wisdom of conscious parenting nurtures the child's true relation-ship with the body, the mind, the world of experience and its Essence. For the parent, the newborn may also represent their teacher, since the infant's openness resonates as wholeness within the parent. A parent can look through their child's virgin eyes and remember that the world is fresh and new. The child demonstrates that the unknown is wondrous, not something to be feared. The conscious parent can honor the Heart wisdom of the child and can confirm that "I" is really the Heart of God, rather than the limitation of form. When the parent is free of separation, the child is not objectified and a life free of lack is nurtured. A child is naturally Now and has no focus on the past or the future, therefore a conscious parent fosters this reality. Free of the parents' programmed concepts and beliefs, the child cherishes its inner security of the Changeless, plus benefits from spontaneous creativity and intelligence, while unconditional love and peace thrive. The tide of conditioning in the culture, the media and the schools is definitely strong; hence the knowing parent points toward the recognition of the Heart within their child's peers as none other than its own, regardless of their peers unconscious behavior. Consequently, the child silently offers true compassion and forgiveness in lieu of opposition in the face of their peers' resistance. Harmony and truth are innate and manifest effortlessly, when not conceptualized. Wholeness is naturally present at birth and only needs nurturing. Conditioning can only conceal wholeness, not enhance it.

We can only sense the dramatic impact on the world, if children were born to conscious families, free of the idea of the fall from the Garden and then enter a conscious school environment. It would enter school as the teacher of wisdom, not by speaking, but by simply being present. Being present, the child would study and learn more effectively the practical knowledge that is required for successful living, but remain free of the conditioning and habituation of separation and fear. The child's presence would sustain emotional intelligence and remain free of the conceptual dream.

You are one of many grown children, who were taught and conditioned to believe in the separate image of "I." Now is the time for inner exploration and its revelation. By eliminating the original separation, the fall from the Garden is revealed to have been an illusion and you enjoy heavenly and worldly seeing, as one sight. We are one life living and we are an "awake" intelligence. Identification with "I," this pronoun of personal suffering and its limitation to the physical form are delusions, all of which dissolve in Essence.

"Dreaming I"

Everything that you are currently distinguishing in your field of awareness is an object in your visualized world. You probably perceive these objects as being separate from you. For example, close your eyes and imagine a lovely bird perched in a palm tree along an aqua blue ocean.

Since direct experience is essential, pause for a moment to envision this tranquil scene in detail.

These imagined objects are appearing in your world of imagination. They are what I refer to as object consciousness. You were probably visualizing that the bird was separate from the tree and that both were separate from the ocean. Furthermore, it is likely that you were experiencing all of them as separate from you. Separation is the essence of the daytime dream of duality. Waking up from the daytime dream is the essence of enlightenment.

Continuing our experiment, draw your attention away from the imagined objects to sit for a moment with the one who is imagining. Just relax and be the imaginer, without imagining anything. Be alert and feel your inner world.

You are the subject of all the separate objects that you have imagined. You imagined the bird. You imagined the tree. You imagined the ocean. Finally, you even imagined you. In this last example, you imagined yourself, as another object within your field of awareness. The objectified "I" and the objects of imagination compose the daytime dream, whereas you are the field of Awareness. When you stop dividing and perceiving yourself as an object, it is impossible to dream that you are separate from the Heart. Awakening extinguishes object consciousness, including the objectified "I." Without dreaming "I," fear and desire disappear. Instead, you realize the wholeness in the joy of being.

Imagining Separation

Identified with the body, you are dreaming that you are the thinker and identification with the thinker maintains separation. You then are limited to mental experience. The thinker can only dream separation, since separation is all that the individual thinker knows. Through imagination alone, it theoretically splits from wholeness and mentally establishes a concept that refers to a separate Source. This split breeds fear that is embodied as madness, hostility, resentment, sadness, jealousy, competition, insecurity, dishonesty, anger, rage and bondage. Further, it breeds the desire for better survival, always greater power, more relative happiness, acquisition, achievement, attainment, sexual obsession and conceptualized freedom. In the dream world of separation, the thinker constantly desires to get something from someone else or believes that someone else should provide this or that to satisfy its sense of lack. This desire for gain is actually a desire for wholeness, in order to fulfill the lack caused by the self-created concept of separation. Simply, separation is partial and can never be whole. Concurrently, the thinker is fearful that someone might take something away, so it fixates on the threat of loss. Even relative happiness is insecure, since it is temporary and can be stolen. For ego, threat lurks everywhere. The attributes of duality are unquenchable desire and ceaseless fear, which obviously cause suffering. This suffering is the consequence of "dreaming I" and this misfortune is the fate of unawareness. The thinker's suffering and its self-projected agony onto the world are not caused by any other person, object or situation. It is unnecessarily sourced within the mind-made self. For the identified thinker, who is seeking fulfillment, the only real alternative is to wake up from the dream of form. The fact that you experience separation, isolation, loneliness, alienation, or any other variation of human suffering is because you have mentally separated from Totality. Of course, separating from Totality is impossible, since it is total. Duality is a delusion of the unawake mind. I am not "me" plus "myself." I am "I" alone. There are not two. As you begin to awaken, attention shifts away from the dream world to the objectified "I" and we find that it does not exist. Since I am not the dream body in the world of form, what does the mental concept "I" reference? Where is it pointing? The pathway is through the inner body into formlessness.

Is Anyone Really Here?

To imagine the culmination of your identity as personal might seem quite dreadful to some. After all, we worked so hard to develop ourselves. We have achieved so much, acquired exhaustively and surely will become so much more. Or maybe we have failed so many times, lost so much and surely will become even less. Of whom are we speaking? Who is that? My question for you, "Is anyone really here?" Please do not answer without investigation, since that would be a conditioned response. Pause for a moment and look inside as we undergo another experiment.

Relaxing, please close your eyes and be aware of your gentle breathing. Then silently ask, "Who am I?" After asking the question, with the mind open to the unknown, listen attentively for an answer. If a thought comes up in reply, ask the question again, being as alert as you might be if you were listening to a burglar who had just entered your home. Go ahead and pause for a moment to inquire, "Who am I?"

What did you find? Is anyone really here? In working with people, they usually laugh and sigh in relief. At last, there are no more stories or images to maintain. You are free and there is no separate self. Therefore, what is being lost in waking up from the personal dream of lack? We have only the idea of suffering to lose. "Dreaming I" is a myth. Follow the "I" thought back to its Source. From where does it arise? The image of "I" is nothing more than an empty word, the depth of which you may not have explored. Imagine! There is no separate self and yet we have tried to build a successful, loving life upon the concept. To realize your true identity, you inquire more deeply. When you inquire within, you find the space of gentle being. This being is not personal and it is not form. In truth, it is the greater life that is alive in you. This becomes conscious, only when you are present to *living*, instead of being what you do. The Essence of this delicate being is the divine dimension that arises within you, when you are in conscious alignment with simply being.

It is a joy to discover that the beginning assumption of "me" was all wrong in the first place. That mental image is a mere concept and you are infinitely more! Your lifetime purpose is to awaken to this dimension of formlessness. You are the greater life's purpose and when you are present to living, you are an open window for unconditional love to flow into the universe. The daytime dream of duality and its suffering are pointing to the belief of the mind-made self as your identity. The discovery of nothing personal is not a diminishment of your being. In the release of the personal, it is realized that you are the Essence of Pure Being, within which all form is contained. You are not an insignificant speck within the field of Totality. You are the greater life and have no need for protection and gain. When the mind-made self constructs protective armor, you then experience isolation from others and from your Essence. With good fortune, you become conscious of this identity crisis and this is the turning point toward home. The pathway may lead to the Essence of enlightenment.

The mind-made self has limited vision and irreverently reduces everyone and everything into fragments to be used as a means to an end. It gives birth to endless desires and to the never-ending fear of lack. No matter how many desires the separate self fulfills and how many fears it tries to escape, there will always be more, since fractions can never be whole. The only solution is to realize our true wholeness as the Essence of formlessness. It satisfies all desire and conquers all fear. You are the Essence of *Awake Joy* and it is time to wake up from this daytime dream to realize that you are awake.

When living in identification with mind-made self, life can seem meaningless. Unfortunately, the best possible relationship that this self-concept can have with family, Life and the world is an object-to-object relationship. Two empty concepts cannot know one another. Their relationship is based upon a dream of separation, need and insecurity. In misidentification with the false sense of self, we are hiding from the joy that we are seeking.

Wake Up to Wakefulness

Essence is simply not an object and therefore, the conceptual mind cannot know its Essence. Essence is not an experience or state that comes and goes within the world of form. It is permanent and free of experience. We can only *be* Essence and yet, it remains untouched. When we surrender the duality created by the separate self and its body reference point, the non-dual is realized as wakefulness. This discovery occurs without expectation or effort and has no requirement or standard. Nonetheless, awakening used to be extremely rare. Today, this is not so and people are opening to this reality. Awakening is emerging everywhere through so many expressions of life. We are finally discovering the true Essence of the human being and that Essence is the Pure Being of the human, beyond the limitations of conditioned thought and the identification with form. We are not our name, thoughts, emotions or physical form. When we stop searching and resonate as still being Grace naturally emerges, just as the morning sunlight gently parts the clouds.

Enlightenment is unlike traditional teachings, where the subject matter is learned and then mentally conceptualized. Instead, we awaken to what is here and now, when the concepts, beliefs and assumptions of conditioned thought are relinquished. We are then free of an imaginary future, which means being free of intention, anticipation, attainment, expectation and the becoming process. We are liberated from the imagined continuity of the past and its related storyline. At last, we wake up to wakefulness and realize true freedom.

If the mind-made self is asleep, that is to say unconscious, it is like a reactionary puppet that dances toward or flees away from whatever it desires or fears. For a puppet, there is no escape, since a puppet can never be freed from the puppeteer. The concept of a separate puppeteer is a figment of imagination that only seems to exist, because of the misidentification with the non-existent puppet. Now is the time to wake up. The separate self has danced and fled long enough. We are the alive and sentient Essence. Focus attention on being the immovable doorway of Now, rather than the movable content of the present moment.

When we realize timelessness, we are then open to the creative flow of life, instead of being distracted by the separate self and its ideas. Our Essence is pure loveliness and we are unified and harmonious. I am inviting you to glimpse your radiant magnificence. There is only the Essence. You and everything that you see and everything that you cannot see are only the Essence. The entire universe is within you and you are the universe. The infinity of space is reflecting the infinity of the Essence within you. Awakening is ultimately realizing the eternal Essence as *Awake Joy* and subsequently embodying this Essence in living. Your departure from wakefulness is only a dream. There is only wakefulness. You are free to imagine yourself otherwise, but you cannot be other than you truly are.

Fear and all of its variations are ego's possessions. It is projecting a movie, so to speak, and when we turn up the lights, we see that the channel does not need changing. Essence is consciousness appearing as all the varied forms, while never losing its essential formlessness. We are deathless, since this formlessness is the Eternal Life. Whether consciousness is with or without form, consciousness itself never changes. Essence is timelessly awake and we now have the opportunity to realize this transcendental wakefulness. Wake up to the Essence. Wake up to wakefulness. There is an alarm sounding within you. You are welcome to rollover, turn the alarm off and continue snoozing for eons. On the other hand, you are also welcome to recognize that this penetrating alarm is a call from the Awakened and snooze no more. If you hear this call, I invite you to stay awake. The Awake Life is fully integrated and thus without differentiation. It is copasetic, harmonious and spontaneous. Who you are is the Essence of Being that is perceiving and the graceful ballet of purely functioning.

Chapter Five

Innocence

"Suddenly, there was innocence, so simple, so clear and delicate. It was a meadow of innocence past all pleasure and ache, beyond all torture of hope and despair. It was there and it made the mind, one's whole being innocent; one was of it; past measure, past word, the mind transparent and the brain young without time."

~ Jiddhu Krishnamurti

Amy's Innocence

During a morning walk, a three year old ran up to me on the beach, stopped and gazed into my eyes with wide-eyed innocence. She smiled without shyness or restraint. Soon, without saying a word, she dashed away, running with the wind, as her brunette curls tossed in the warm breeze. The gust dissipated for a moment, so she abruptly turned and ran back, with the same glee and vivacious exuberance. Already identifying, labeling, categorizing and imitating, she shared that her name was Amy, as she pointed with her forefinger to her petite form. She bubbled with enthusiasm as she called my attention to "a *little* wave, a great *big* wave and a *little, teeny, tiny* baby wave," with the same intonation as *Goldilocks and the Three Bears*. The breeze picked her up again and she scurried away giggling, without a thought of looking back. Amy was in the current of Life.

From the joy in Amy's eyes shined the light of uninhibited love. In total surrender, she spontaneously shifted the direction of her running, with the changes in the wind. Her animation and childlike effervescence are rarely encountered in adults. As adults, we adore children Amy's age for their innocence and openness. They live fearlessly in the unknown with an exceptional sense of aliveness, fascination and adventure. Their openness is loveable.

Through the conditioning of life, we become resistant, closed and untrusting. We would like to blame life, but this is the fate of ego identification and the blind acceptance of separation. If we find openness so loveable, why do we resist, contract and close down? What are we trying to protect? Only a false image needs protection, so perhaps it is safe to let down our guard, in order to be free of the past. We are identified with the ego and therefore live mentally within past time. It appears that we are trying to protect ourselves from being hurt by love, simultaneously longing for love and all the while *being* love. This is a regrettable enigma. Amy was free of the past and was naturally expressing the joy of living. Although perhaps unconscious of it, she was experiencing the Essence of *Awake Joy*.

The Mirror is Self-Revealing

"Dreaming I" lives the life situation within one dimensional thought. When it experiences an unfavorable circumstance, it judges, categorizes and then stores the memory for future use. Then, it thinks about it. Like a photo album, it reruns the ill-fated images again and again. Anger and force gain momentum with each rerun. The suffering self might even replay the "movie" with different endings. It imagines what it should have said or practices what it will say next time. It tries to keep the story alive and needs an enemy to oppose, since this opposition makes the ego feel real and alive. Through resistance, it gains the illusion of more power to fortify its perceived weakness. Concurrently, it may fear the delusion of its existence.

Once it tires of the mental reruns, it starts reliving the story by disrespectfully sharing it with its family and friends. Through mental repetition, the event has escalated to grand proportions and the face of the victimizer has grown uglier. The "dreaming I" indirectly encourages its acquaintances to judge the circumstances, not recognizing that their judgment can only be as truthful as their conditioned point of view, their past judgment and whatever they perceive that they might need or get in the future. Nonsensically, the ego is happy if its friends and family agree with its side of the story. It might even get angry with them, if they do not. In this case, it may relate more stories about the enemy in an attempt to coerce a disbeliever that it was right all along.

Each repeat of the story reinforces the past conditioning and intensifies its pain, as it further engrains its victim image. As the negative whirlpool deepens, the magnetism may draw more victimizers, until its misidentification and conditioning are finally made conscious. This is the harsh, inevitable activity of the unawake mind. Instead of suffering, you have the opportunity to look into the mirror of life and notice that it is self-revealing. It is pointing to the false image of ego, its concept of separation and misidentification with form. The ego adores the game of storytelling, since it is afraid of feeling insignificant. Therefore, it imagines the need for more power as it clothes itself with stronger defenses for future use. Eventually, it may even generalize the actions of a few, into the judgment against an entire class, such as "men." Now, it must not only protect itself from a few specific enemies, but also an entire army in the future. Playing this game involves an unending loss of innocence that results in further isolation and loneliness. Of course, true Innocence cannot be lost, since it is inherently who we are. However, the ego dreams that it is no longer free to run about like Amy.

Finally, "dreaming I" begins to recognize that this self-revealing mirror is actually pointing back to the mind-made self. Attention shifts inside and it observes the inner rampage against itself, through self-judgment and self-criticism. Without focusing on the enemy in the life story, it observes the more brutal, mental battlefield in the head. It begins recognizing that it is its own worst enemy. Without this recognition, the past-future cycle succeeds again. It recycles until it realizes how its misidentification with the mental conditioning is perpetuating its suffering. Initially, such trickery of thought is inescapable. However, if you remain presently still and observe within, without identified involvement, the trickster named ego is finally exposed and dissolved. It is revealed that both the victim and the victimizer have their roots of illusion within your mental ideas. This is a good time for self-compassion and patience. By repeatedly bringing awareness back to itself, you begin to recognize that you have always been free of the repetitive past-future cycle and never contained. You realize the illusion of the false sense of "me" and its concepts. As Presence, which is your still attention, your awareness sharply focuses. You are freed from the illusion of past-future time, where ego resides. Free of time, you begin having glimpses of the inner Field of Innocence. If you continue to be attentive and mostly time-free, thought begins to lose momentum and the joy of being consciously emerges. You become luminous, through which the reflection of Innocence shines. The Field begins *true* Self-revealing. The hazy vapor on the mirror of life clears and you recognize the sacredness of Innocence, which contains all appearances. Life may now seem pristine and reverent.

The entire cycle of past-future fear and victimization is a dream of the misidentified consciousness and its mental separation. When "dreaming I" judges a circumstance as dreadful, its judgment causes an inner reaction of resistance. It suffers due to its judgmental thoughts, which are all based on its past experience. Whatever the circumstance, it is torturing itself by reliving the past. It is critical of the enemy in the life situation, yet it relives the self-tyranny again and again. What was already cruel from its personal point of view becomes crueler. The residue of past pain continues to accumulate and may even begin to harm the body.

If your wish is to be free of suffering, you must stop terrorizing yourself and others. When you stay sharply present and free of time, the "I" thought does not arise, since it requires time. Being present defies the false image of ego and therefore defies mental separation. If you slip into time and the image of "I" does arise, do not touch it. If you do not identify, it just floats by harmlessly. If you do identify, you will sense unease in the form of negativity. This signals you to bring awareness back to itself. Pain dissolves and you regain the peace that underlies all fixations.

Emotional pain is an energy field that attracts like kind as it projects onto the mirror of life. The self-revealing mirror is consciousness pointing toward that which is being overlooked within you, i.e. misidentification with the past image of "I," separation and emotional attachment to pain. While lost in the dream, you project similar circumstances into the future. You are moving in a senseless circle, from the past to future pain and back to the pain of more past. The Field of Now is completely overlooked, while drowning in the past-future whirlpool. As the Now, nothing is broken and nothing needs to be fixed for you are whole and pure. Life is forever new, innocent and enhanced with a fresh sense of adventure. You are free of the robotic cycle. On the other hand, while you are reliving the past and practicing for the future, you are missing the joy of being. Your opportunity is to remain still and keenly present, free of past and future, while all else comes and goes. Free of resistance, the Current of Life runs consciously through you.

Within the context of your mental and emotional conditioning, one concept after another is added to your defense mechanisms. Lost in your identification with thought, your child-like passion dwindles. Life loses its levity and weariness slithers in. You forget that memory is only another concept, a mental representation of a past appearance. The representation has no life or substance and yet you demonstrate emotional attachment. Once conditioned, the ego is on the lookout and expects similar frightful circumstances at any given moment. It is scoping an imagined future, with the eyes of the past and blind to what truly is. Of course, the dream life in the mirror obligingly provides the dream that you believe in most.

When ego recognizes a circumstance that reinforces its separating cause, it is as though it takes a snapshot. Just as we take a photo of something that we enjoy while on vacation, the snapshot does not represent the entire experience, since it is selective. Ego discriminates and attaches to the tiny segment of circumstance that matches the image for which it is looking; namely another opportunity to suffer. Then, it looks at the same dull and boring photographs over and over. Furthermore, it continues to complain, lest we forget and just innocently be. Memory snapshots are not even accurate, since the event is viewed through a veil of past conditioning. The veil is the flawed belief in individuality as identity. This separation produces a sense of threat, which causes us to push people away or cling to them. Most irreverently, we reduce others to mere objects, from which we need to either get or take something. Even more disheartening, we may begin projecting onto others, that they are actually the ones who are pushing or cling- ing for some ego cause. While projecting and reacting in this manner, innocent relationship, which is free of time, is avoided. The ego requires time and within time, true relationship cannot thrive. Truth reveals that a separate self does not exist and that is what ego fears most. The mirror of consciousness reflects either your egotistic illusions or the Self-revealing Innocence of Essence.

Consciousness is the Mirror

Eventually, we take responsibility for the mirror of life. Since the mirror of object consciousness consistently points to what remains unexposed within us, we listen to our mind label and qualify the world. What we are labeling is not in the world. The world is within us. So, we follow the image in the mirror back to what is being pointed toward within us. Through self-observation, what we were holding unconsciously is exposed and freed. In each release, the mirror reflects clearer seeing. What is requesting our attention is being revealed before us in every moment. Your teacher is with you everywhere, not only within, but also as the mirror of life. Unfortunately, we carelessly take the mirror for granted and dismiss it as ordinary life.

Relatively speaking, you *are* the images in the mirror. When you notice inner resistance to a life situation, investigate to observe the unconscious thoughts that are causing your feeling of unease. This is the past alive in you. When you are free of time, the life circumstance is free of your overlay of illusion. Instead of manipulating the life circumstance, which is ultimately impossible, discover who resists. That one is the ego, the conditioned false sense of "me." Conditioning is something that you learned in the past and habituation is never now. The ego only seems to exist in the illusion of past time. It is *known* and that which is known is past. Only the Unknown is Now. You have the opportunity to surrender the resistance, which means *not knowing* and not knowing is a return to Innocence.

When you surrender and accept what is, there is a relaxation of energy. You regain tranquility and the quietude of mind. In the resisting movement of conditioned thought, the reflection in the mirror is distorted. Of course, the reflection is still consciousness, but the images are shaded. One could say that the mind's vision is dimmed. I suppose that it is somewhat similar to wearing sunglasses, except the vision is impaired, rather than enhanced. Papaji was one of India's most cherished sages and one of his favorite analogies was that of mistaking a rope for a snake. By analogy, in the darkness of the movement of mind within time, while observing a snake, one fearfully reacts. However, in the stopping of the mind, the light of consciousness reveals that the snake was really only a rope. In the stillness of the radiant mind, Awareness shines through reflecting the sacred Innocence of its unbound nature.

The Field of Consciousness

Your opportunity is to compassionately embrace all that appears as Essence. You could be humble in welcoming and honoring the images in the mirror. Instead of resistance and reaction, you could reflect the truth of Essence, which is Innocence. One could say that a distorted image is nothing more than a field test, to see if you still have the past tendency to "take bait," in order to nourish the false sense of self. Conditioned existence is a dream. It is a dream, within the mirror of object consciousness, which is being dreamt by a conceptually identi- fied dreamer. The mirror is pointing to the continued illusion of duality. However, there is no need for active change. As Presence, you simply remain the open and free awareness, unidentified with content. The transformation of the mirror happens by itself, as you remain true to who you really are. These shadowed images, which you misconstrue as your personal reality, have only the power that you attribute to them. Life seems dull and exhausting when you are lost in the world of sym- bols, inaccurate representations and heavier and heavier armor. As past mental representations are surrendered, the opportunity for awakening draws near. Like Amy, you regain your child-like exuberance and then realize the unfathomable dimension of wakefulness.

During the transformation process, many words assume new definitions. For instance, before awakening, the word "love" may have possessed a connotation that is the opposite of hate. After awakening, love refers to true Love that is supreme and unconditional. True Love has no opposite. It is transcendent or free of the love-hate cycle, which means that it embraces the illusion of the cycle, all the while being Supreme Love. Transcendental Love is changeless, even as life changes. It never diminishes to hate and is free of the cause and condition of relative love. Likewise, Innocence takes on a new connotation. When I speak of Innocence, I am not referring to the innocence that is defined in relationship to guilt. Innocence is transcendental, as it pertains to the Field. The Field of Innocence is virginal, as in the sense of being pristine. It is perfection prior to form and embraces the mental illusion of the innocent-guilt cycle. Innocence remains forever untouched and is your innermost, sacred core. This changeless Field is waiting to consciously emerge into your life situation. I am not suggesting that you need to learn how to be innocent again. No, there is nothing to learn and nothing to become. The Field is perfectly within you now and ever-present. No matter what life situation that you have had to endure, true Innocence cannot be tarnished. This Field is indestructible, radiantly vital and all-pervasive. As formlessness, consciousness permeates all form. You transcend and embrace *All that Is* and remain impervious to conditioned existence.

When you are identified with the thinker, you are not consciously aware of the Field. As the thinking ego is exposed and relinquished, you begin glimpsing the transcendental, as it reflects outside as life. In other words, the mirror of life is Self-revealing Innocence. The culprits that appear to conceal this luminous Field are misidentification with me, the concept of separation and identification with the body. When the Field seems to be concealed, it does not mean that the innocent Radiance is not here. It is only temporarily concealed, behind the clouds of misidentification, attachment, judgment and any number of various conditionings, all of which belong to the idea of "me." Come out and be seen. Attempting to hide from your-Self is futile.

For Self-discovery, you become aware of your conditioning. You begin by turning the mind inward toward the Heart. Be still and aware of your inner world. Listen to the mental chaos dispassionately and innocently, without involvement. Then, shift attention to the stillness of being that lies deeper. The content of the thought does not matter. I am not asking you to change the thought process or even resist it. Changing the conditioning is only more thought. It reinforces the illusive power of an imaginary ego, itself only a mental construct. Furthermore, it is an act of self-inflicted pain. Simply be present and honorably notice that all of the thoughts and judgments come and go, while you remain still and changeless. In Presence, the conditioned past disappears.

When you become aware of your habits and conditioning, they are surrendered, since when you are *aware* of them, you are already beyond. Phantom fear may occasionally rattle its ghostly chains for awhile, in an attempt to entice you, but you are no longer fooled. You can even be amused at the sound of the chains. Soon it is absolutely silent and in this silence, you realize your essential nature. Being present, you are free of the conceptual imprisonment of identification and training, as they melt like ice cubes in the sun and evaporate. The power of this sun is the Field of Now. Daytime may exhibit ever-changing weather conditions, but the changing conditions do not alter the fact that it is daytime. The transcendental being is enduring like daytime; whereas life situations change and have no true power over joy.

Within you, the Field is free of psychological defense and attack. It is free of experience and yet it is the Field upon which all experience is played. Innocently, every moment is a new play of creation, unless you hang on to past-future fear or desire and miss it. Clinging to the past, you experience the reruns. Free of the past, you have the fascination of innocent play. When you are free of the deception of time, you are free of the self-perpetuating cycle. Past and future dissolve as the Now shines clear. When forms appear, they have no past. For instance, even to greet your mother at the door, as the *image* of mother, carries a multitude of past stories and future projections. Look inquisitively to see who is appearing. Is it your mother or is it really a projection of *you* appearing within the mirror? For once, not knowing is the correct answer. When you recognize and realize that you are innocent, you can only offer Innocence. You have no one to defend and no one to attack; nothing sticks. To whom would it stick? It is similar to being transparent and life just freely flows through you. You prosper from the deliciousness of being nobody and are free of the burden of being somebody. Somebody plays the game of defense and attack on the Field. Nobody is simply being free and others are spared your guilt-ridden projections. Having realized that you are the Field of Innocence, you just do not play the game anymore.

Without forethought or judgment, you are then spontaneously animated to right action. Right action is pure functioning and it arises through total surrender. In unequivocal surrender, you do not know how you may be used by Truth, nor give significance to being animated as this or that, since it does not matter. You have pure knowing that right action is the appropriate mirror for the perfect cause and condition, which innocently remains a mystery. Unworthiness is an attribute of a lack of innocence, so all life is recognized as equally worthy. This equanimity is tranquil and peaceful, no matter how life appears. In appearance, some images may be clothed in loveliness and others in cruelty. Regardless of how one is pretending to dress up, conscious-ness remains open, unprotected and free, while the Field animates the innocent, yet ruthless, play of life.

Chapter Six

The Truth of Renunciation

"When you want something other than these attachments and relationships, they naturally fall off by themselves. You are not to break them, but they themselves will fall like a wall of sand."

~ Papaji

Ramana and the Buddha

Seekers of spiritual enlightenment often hear the term "renunciation." In India, a spiritual seeker is called a "sadhu." The seeker renounces all relationships, abandons possessions and ignores care of the body, in the belief that this type of renunciation will facilitate enlightenment. Ramana Maharshi, who lived in India and who is one of the world's most cherished sages, pointed out that since the Essence of enlightenment was not within circumstantial life; one could realize the true Self anywhere, regardless of the life situation. He encouraged that this type of renunciation was not required.

While growing up, Buddha's family protected him by confining him to the palace. As a prince, he possessed wealth, fame and honor.

He was conditioned to believe that only abundance, youth and good health existed. They protected Buddha from knowing that the body was temporary and susceptible to disease and death. They guarded him from envisioning poverty. Still, Buddha became discontent and restless. He escaped the boundaries of the palace to explore life outside its walls. He was dismayed and disillusioned in the discovery that there was poverty, that good health was vulnerable to disease and that in disease or old age, the body dies. Outside the palace walls, he peered into the faces of pain and suffering. Buddha was stunned by the meaninglessness of a physical life that could end abruptly at any moment in death. He left his elegant palace life, possessions and family. He renounced everyone and everything to discover the meaning and purpose of life. Buddha became a seeker of enlightenment.

He went to teachers, who taught various practices and encouraged austerities to gain enlightenment. Buddha finally surrendered the teachers, when he ascertained that enlightenment could not be provided externally by anyone. Still renouncing the care of the body, he then entered the forest and sat under the Bodhi Tree in silent attention. At last, he surrendered the austerities in the realization that enlightenment meant being free from identification and matters of the mind. Enlightenment was beyond the mind and the external renunciation provoked by thought was meaningless. The renunciation required for enlightenment is renouncing the unaware mind.

Renunciation is Being Now

Worldly renunciation is not required for enlightenment. Even in the solitude of a forest, the stillness beneath the silence would be overlooked, if you had the noise of compulsive thought in your head. The outward conditions for awakening are of no significance. The renunciation required for awakening is the renunciation of the identified thinker. Free of the thinker, identification with thought is impossible, so conditioned thought loses its significance. The "possessions" of thought, belief and assumption are effortlessly relinquished by resting in silent being. Without the detachment from the thinker, awakening eludes the seeker. This detachment is not a "doing." By being Now, you are intensely alert, but also relaxed. In this resting attention, thought does not arise, unless it is required as a useful tool. Even the thought "I" remains within Source, which makes identification with objects impossible. Being Now is free of all matters of the mind. It contains these matters, but remains unidentified. Being Now is the truth of renunciation, since you are free of everything worldly, including the thinker and all of its attachments.

Upon investigation, you cannot find yourself anywhere within the mind, so you stop searching. Any movement from here and now is a movement away from the beauty that you are. Someone might find it a convenient mind strategy to proclaim that they must renounce their family and home to find Truth. This mind game is called co-opting and there is no winner to this game. Truth cannot be co-opted or used. If you hear the inner words, "I need to leave to find '*my*' self" or "I need to leave to find '*my*' purpose," it is a pointer toward co-opting. "Me and mine" are the roots of suffering and ego's mark. The Self is not "myself." Furthermore, the Self is here now, as you. The purpose of life is not "my" purpose. Life is its own purpose and you are *That*. There is no "my-self." All is the Self. Anyway, where would you go to renounce an omnipresent Field of Awareness called Totality? Where must you go to discover Now?

Ego Speaks of Renunciation

Only the ego believes that it possesses something to renounce. Who is the possessor? No one possesses and no one renounces. There is no image of "I," with an individual consciousness. All is Pure Consciousness. Once you accept the qualification and limitation of ego, whose existence is an illusion, you must then renounce "I," the body, the world, attachments, fears, problems, worries, pleasures, past, future and the doer, just to name a few. If you are free of the qualification of "I," what remains? It can be so simple. Being Now, you are free of both external content and internal thought and concepts.

If you are willing to dismantle the conditioned thought structures of ego in attention to what really is, you will find that there is no one here and that there is nothing to surrender, while compulsive thinking dissolves. Through self-observation, you rest as still permanence and anything impermanent, such as thought, simply comes and goes. Thoughts just float by in the thought stream and soon disperse into the silent depth of Pure Being. The ego is nothing more than learned attributes and conditioned thoughts. If you are not the ego, then who are you? This is the *only* essential question. Your problems and worries do not belong to you. As long as you maintain that they do, you remain helpless and happiness remains hopeless. Surrender them to Grace. All needs are met from within. Only the ego has something to surrender, get, lose, or renounce. Truly, what is there to renounce, if the one who renounces is non-existent?

For enlightenment, you transcend the body-mind. It is insignificant whether you imagine having possessions, family, home and body or whether you imagine not having possessions, family, home and body. The difference is inconsequential. Transcendence is moving beyond both having and not having. You stop all of the doing and not doing in the mind and realize that there is no doer. This does not mean that you sit stagnantly doing nothing. This is another mind strategy of co-opting. It means that when you look directly in attention, there is no one doing. All is happening by itself. What freedom this is! You recognize that you have always been surrendered to Life and it animates you in functioning. There is only functioning and everything else is imagination.

There is no practitioner to practice or not practice. The transcendental being is free of both and you are That. You can use body awareness or any other type of alertness, as a portal to transcendence. The answer is not the type of activity that appears in your awareness. The portal is being the aware Now. In fact, it is impossible to be other than here and now. Are you in the past right now? Will you ever be in the past? Are you in the future right now? Will you ever be? No, you are always here and now. In the end, your identification with your body-mind is relinquished, since it is directly experienced that anything chased within the mind, emotions or body is limited and impermanent. Surely, it can be recognized that the limited cannot contain the unlimited and that impermanence cannot contain permanence. This does not mean that body, thought and emotion are not honored. It simply means that your Essence lies beyond.

Renunciation is not a pushing away of thought. This is resistance and actually accelerates thought. You will find that anything that is resisted perpetuates. Renunciation means to remain still and present without effort, while being Now. Thoughts do not belong to you, unless you identify and attach. They remain simple thought forms that are no longer personal. Without the one who identifies, thoughts are free and so are you.

Nothing external or internal is required for enlightenment other than to be conscious of Being. People have many excuses about why they cannot be happy. The discovery of living joy is in spite of every excuse. For enlightenment, it does not matter whether you are presently happy or unhappy. It does not matter if you are a student, a busy mother, or employed in an office with long hours. It does not matter, whether you are having too much fun or immersed in boredom. Living joy is in spite of everything. Your option is to wake up from the dream of concepts to realize Awake Life. Humanity's misery is a dream, within the illusion of your own misery of separation. The living answer is within you.

Chapter Seven

The End of Time

> *"The personal self by its very nature is constantly pursuing pleasure and avoiding pain. The ending of this pattern is the ending of the self. The ending of the self with its desires and fears enables you to return to your real nature, the source of all happiness and peace."*
>
> ~ Sri Nisargadatta Maharaj

Ego's Story-Time

Thought seems to begin in one moment and after certain duration, it ends in another. This gives the impression of thought's movement through space. We define this sequential progression as time. However, the timeless Essence of being is not in movement at all. It is absolutely immovable and free of space altogether. The gift of this motionless dimension is that consciousness has the play of motion. You would not even be able to perceive progression, without the still background that sustains it. Without the light of consciousness, you would not be able to distinguish anything in this dimension, just as nothing would be visible in the heart of night, without the moon's reflecting light.

This imperceptible Essence allows magnificent perceiving. The silence creates the joy of listening, while the invisible manifests exquisite seeing. The untouchable facilitates extraordinary touching, while the scent-free originates superb smelling. Even the tasteless generates the marvel of tasting. In short, Essence initiates the love of form, in order for consciousness to experience. Ultimately, experience transcends, in order for the Essence to consciously meet itself. And yes, its immovability creates the delusion of time, which produces suffering, so that you may wake up to the truth of joy. This apparent limitation points only to the Infinite.

Memory is recalling a past mental image, which occurred within chronological time. Once the incident has transpired, it innocently remains nothing more than a notch on a historical dateline. In other words, the mental image is no longer a current affair. It merely remains a mental image. After a circumstance is judged as negative, the dilemma seems to be that we become a storyteller about the emotional impact of the mental image. Initially, processing our feelings might be quite helpful. However even as adults, many are still retelling a painful childhood story or a tale about a former mate, an unfair job situation or other aching memory. In our willingness to endlessly repeat a hurtful story, we are keeping our pain alive and thereby experience recurrent suffering. The past mental image itself is harmless, even in its original pain. Ultimately, we cannot keep our painful story and get rid of the pain.

When the ego believes that it has learned something psychologically, it crystallizes the experience by creating a story. Storytelling is an enduring reinforcement for our past torment. Please recognize that the storyteller is none other than the ego, which can only seem to exist within time. This storyteller is the actual root of your lingering misery.

Even though the false sense of self mourns that it cannot escape, its fixation on the pain of the past can only ensure more torture. What motive might the ego have in mind, so to speak? The ego's self-serving strategy is that it needs this story in order to maintain the delusion of its existence. Without the story, we would quickly recognize that there is no ego. We would also observe that we are truly timeless and already free of the pain. In the power of timelessness, you are already perfection.

Without your storyteller, where is your story?

Freedom from the past cannot be found by centering on the pain of the past. Your freedom is not even in healing the past. This concentration is a past fixation, so you are not present for joy. Time freedom cannot be found within time. It cannot take more time to take you out of time. Only Presence is free of time and ego cannot survive in Presence. Free of the ego, you are free of ego's affliction and required storyline.

Even ego's desire to change the past creates the illusion of present lack and therefore creates misery. By tending ego, you are not being present and robotically project an imaginary future that is based on a memorized past. This focal point re-creates what you are trying to escape. Even your desire to repeat the pleasure of a past story at a future time is creating the inference of present lack. The result is an accumulation of pain. This is simple. Within time, there is suffering. In timelessness, there is joy.

Psychological conditioning is not practical discovery that simply results in the acquisition of valuable knowledge. An example of practical discovery is when you touch fire for the first time and realize that it is hot. Practically, you have obtained useful knowledge, so that you do not touch fire again. On the other hand, psychological conditioning is when one adds a repetitive narrative about the emotional impact of touching fire. This repetition causes chronic fear, without present danger. Through ego's story-time, you suffer not only the original physical burn, but psychologically suffer every time that you repeat the story. You experience an emotional pain that is not sourced in present reality. Storytelling is self-inflicted agony. Through timelessness, you have the opportunity to stop telling the story, both to yourself and others, in order to free painful memories. You are then here to be aware of past conditioning as it arises. This conditioning is a result of past pain and only appears to be alive in you.

The Ground of Now

Today, the unawake mind has an insatiable infatuation with dreaming "I." In a gathering of unenlightened minds, you witness endless personal storytelling and very little true listening. People do not recognize that something deeper is actually occurring. The ego is the individual self. I refer to this image as the false sense of self, dreaming "I," mind-made self and pseudo self, or simply the concept of "me." As we have discussed, the ego has no life or subsistence without the story and therefore stories are ego's compensation. The ego does not need to listen. It needs to tell stories, since it does not exist outside the realm of the unawake, time-based mind. "I" is only a thought, a past concept. It is no more than another past mental image, to which we add numerous descriptions and stories. The only benefit of these stories is the maintenance of the false sense of self and its incorrect impression of separation. When you yield to storytelling, ego succeeds and you suffer. Moreover, these stories tend to match what you have been conditioned to believe. As you recount the stories, you unconsciously fortify the pseudo self and its past beliefs.

When the "I" thought emerges in consciousness and subsequently identifies with another mental image, the catalyst is either desire or fear. These likes and dislikes distort memory. The result is confusion and suffering. Your option is to discover the timeless factor in every experience and even the timelessness of every memory. Through self-observation, you relinquish all that you distinguish to be an aspect of mind. You scientifically surrender everything that you observe to be impermanent and in movement. What remains is the emptiness of Essence, the pure light of consciousness that is beyond space and time.

The pseudo image loves telling the stories of where it has been in the past or who it was. It adores sharing the stories of where it hopes to go in the future or who it hopes to be. My question is where and who is it right now? The answer is nowhere and nobody, but you must discover this for yourself. Whether the past or future stories are good or bad is inconsequential. Both require identification with a past image. This delusional relationship with time is the source of psychological pain. Ego perversely enjoys the drama, as well as the resulting pain. The pain is good food for more stories and excellent for ego's self-preservation. It imagines enemies to oppose to boost its mental image, to fortify its pseudo-power and to amplify its separate sense of self. Upon awakening, this persistent opposition plainly demonstrates core fears such as insecurity, helplessness and powerlessness. The psychological image is a continual work in progress, while it fixates on emotional problems and conflicts. Simply, if you wake up to the fantasy of the concept of "me," you are free of the problems and conflicts.

At the deepest level, the ego fears that it does not exist. It fears that it is nothing. The bad news, if you can call it that, is that ego *is* nothing. The good news is that you are not who you think. You are infinitely more! Who is the "myself" featured in your thoughts and your subsequent emotional story of desire and fear?

The conditioned intelligence is limited and projects the known. It utilizes what it believes about the past, thereby re-creating the same. The names and forms may change, but the basic themes remain the same. Just like a dog chasing its tail, it cycles from the past to the future and back again in a vicious circle, until it drops to the ground in exhaustion. When the mind drops in this manner, if even for an instant, it lands on the powerful ground of Now. What an exquisite surprise! The immediate eye-opener is that ego needs time and in this discovery, the ego's mirage evaporates. We are then able to discern that the story was nothing more than a bundle of conditioned thoughts that was solidified by fear and desire. All of which belonged to the primary thought, the conceptual "I." We have engaged in an enormous love-hate relationship with "me" and it is nothing. It is no more than a figment of imagination. This is a shocking revelation! At last, the relationship with yourself, the non-existent self, is surrendered.

Has the study of "me" gone on long enough? Are you prepared to surrender the relationship with yourself to discover who you really are? Are you ready to unequivocally surrender to timelessness? Are you willing to be free of the problematic stories and conflicts? Are you prepared to surrender the storyteller in order to realize joy? If you are, then the only essential question is, "Are you?" If the answer is yes, then *who is That?* If the answer is no, then who is?

When your attention is distracted in time fixation, it is impossible to realize true happiness and the abundance of *no time*. Traditionally, humans believe that no time is a stressful condition, when in fact, it is a relaxation. Is it possible that no time is really just the end of time? Is there ever a shortage of Now in your life? Of course, you certainly have the option to contend with thousands of memories, their stories and their continuing emotional impact. You are also welcome to strategize the resolution of thousands of future fears and desires. On the other hand, you could examine whether this ambitious ego, burdened with its need-based insecurity, even exists. The answer to real freedom is self-understanding. For a clear self-investigation, your attention must be unattached and uninvolved. To know the truth, you curiously observe within to determine what truly is. When the "me" is revealed to be non-existent, the veil of ego is lifted and you gaze into the Bride's eyes of Radiant Life.

Do you know your birth? Do you know your death? Do you know the true purpose of life? Do you know who you are beyond your given name and your body? Do you know your emotions? Do you know your body and mind? Born happy, do you know why are you suffering? Do you really have a past? Can you show me the future? Who are you beyond all doubt? What do you know to be steadfastly true?

True Forgiveness

In the external duality of dreaming "I," forgiveness can sometimes remain only a concept. In other words, the ego may conceptually forgive within the mind, but absolute forgiveness might elude the heart. By relinquishing the personal self-image, you transform the concept of mental forgiveness into the Rapture of the Heart. Then through Presence, you maintain the openness of your inner space moment to moment. True forgiveness has no external requirement, which means that it is free of dependence. It has nothing to do with anyone else or the accompanying story-time. Real forgiveness is the power of timelessness within you that is already free of personal history. Where is the past in the here and now?

When you are free of the *concept* of forgiveness, you are living free. This is not an optimist's hope for the future. It is readily accessible for every human being right now. The problem is not the insanity of a multitude of personal and world problems. The problem is the insanity in the delusion of time, which in turn facilitates the runaway madness of the unawake mind.

Living Free Laboratory

One of the most amazing discoveries of living free is the absence of personal problems. You may instantly deny this, however this is true for you right now. May I invite you into the timeless Living Free Laboratory for an experiment to explore this freedom? In a moment, I will ask you to stop reading, but right now I would like you to be aware of the chair upon which you are sitting. Please feel how securely it is supporting you. Now, I would like to draw attention to your feet and feel how solid the floor feels beneath them. In one long inhale, I would like you to draw the mental energy in your head into the natural openness of the Heart. Fully relax and feel the breath effortlessly breathing the body. Go ahead and put this book down. Feel the simplicity of just being. When you are consciously present, please come back to the lab.

I would like you to ask, "What problem do I have precisely right now?" With the energy still in the Heart and not in the head, go ahead and ask this question. I will meet you back here in a moment.

The above question does not pertain to the past and I am not referring to even five minutes into the future. The question is, "Do you have a problem now?" The answer is no, is it not so? You have enough food and shelter, somewhere to sit and you are breathing. You may have bills to pay in the future, chores to do in fifteen minutes, or many other past or future mental concerns. However, here and now, do you have a problem? There never seems to be a problem right now.

This experiment is over, but just to test our findings, I would like you to continue the experiment on your own. Every time that you get into your car and feel the steering wheel in your hands, please ask, "Do I have a problem right now?" As well, every time that you feel the door knob in your hand, while entering your home, I would like you to inquire, "Do I have a problem right now?" You will consistently find that there is not. The miracle of the "continuous" Now is that problems simply do not seem to enter the Field. This wonder is radical.

During your day, if a problem enters your field of experience, pose the Living Free Laboratory question silently, but pointedly, "Do I have a problem right now?" Feel the question in Heart, which is always Now. The ego is likely to oblige with an affirmative reply, since it resides in time. With attentive inner listening, you move out of time into timelessness. Living free of negativity can be a conscious, consistent reality in your life right now. The key words are conscious and now.

Even what you normally conceive to be the present moment is actually already the past from the standpoint of "me." When you are living in identification with the past image of "I," you have relinquished the Now. In lieu of attending the content of the present, focus your attention on its Now-ness. This ethereal Now-ness is called Presence and it is altogether free of content. Content is the life activity or circumstance that is appearing within Presence. You are then available to be present with what truly is, rather than conceiving what you think is happening, based on a past perspective or judgment. When you are asleep to Presence, the world is a conceptual illusion of ever changing positive or negative conditions. It is no more than a dream. The instant that you identify with the first thought "I," you slip into the dream of time. To be consciously free, bring attention back to itself, which means being free of content. To the Eternal, the illusion of time every now and then is insignificant. It is not so serious, so just realign. Besides, it is always Now.

The End of Time Prophecy

A prophecy is something that we predict will happen in the future, such as the end of time prophecy in the Book of Revelations in the Bible. It is impossible for the end of time to happen within time. The end of time cannot be in the future and can only be right now. One wonders whether this biblical prophecy was misinterpreted, within the realm of the time-based, unawake mind. Perhaps the end of time is simply the end of the delusion of time. This makes sense, does it not? Perhaps, the end of the world is really the end of the dream world. Maybe, it is the end of attachment to the time-based ego, its concept of separation and identification with form. Whatever the case, the end of time does coincide with the culmination of the mind-made self. You no longer need the past to prove separate identity in order to realize wholeness. You no longer need suffering to consciously inquire to discover Truth. You no longer need separation to recognize wakefulness. You no longer need duality for experience. You no longer require the future to provide fulfillment. Instead, you have the opportunity for the mind-shattering shift, from the movement of mind within time to the absolute stillness of the Heart. It offers wholeness instead of separation, joy instead of suffering and total fulfillment right now.

Awake Joy points to the realization of the Heart of Life that is beyond time, which is tantamount to beyond the mind. This is not an Essence that you move toward. It is here now as your true nature. It is a breath-taking, vertical shift from "dreaming I" to the open Heart of all being. It is a simple, yet wondrous transformation, which coincidentally is the end of time, as well as the end of the world, as we have known it.

The Time Laboratory

I would like to ask you to pause for a moment and invite you into the Time Laboratory for an experiment. First, just relax and shift your attention within your body. While resting, be aware of how soft the air feels, as it moves in and out of your nose. Rest until you feel tranquil. If there is movement into time, please readjust attention to here and now. With your eyes closed, I would like you to look intensely for the next thought.

Now, please imagine a past situation that still causes you emotional pain. Watch your thoughts as you relive the event through imagination. Go ahead. I will wait for you here.

Let's take a break for a moment and step out of the Time Lab to be here and now. Be aware of your breathing. If the mind is still doing its past thing, as it does, be more present by using your senses. Can you hear the birds singing outside? Do you see something lovely in your room? How does it feel to be here and now?

While you were imagining, did your mental images and inner dialogue cause emotional pain? Could you feel your body contract as your thoughts triggered emotions? In therapy, you could probably succeed in improving the inner dialogue, which would make the emotions less severe, but negativity might still linger, since you are still maintaining an emotional story about a past mental image. While you cannot change the fact that the event occurred, you can be totally free of the story by being consciously Now. How do you feel?

Let me invite you back into the Time Lab one more time, since I have one more experiment. First, I would like you to imagine a future life situation that you have desired for many years. Second, I would like you to imagine something about the future that you have feared might happen for a long time. Third, while you are imagining, I would like to draw your attention to the impact on your body of the thoughts that you have. Go ahead and put the book down for a moment for this three-part experiment.

Could you hear the mental voice? How does your body react to your thoughts about the future? Were the emotions different than those in the last experiment, when you were imagining the past? What emotions did you feel when you thought about a future desire? How did you feel when you thought about something that you fear might happen? Did the emotions correlate with the thoughts? How did your body feel? Were you aware of any mental images, while you were imagining? How did you feel about these images? Did your thoughts or mental images have anything to do with past pain?

Could you step out of the Time Lab to be powerfully and completely here now? Be aware of your breathing and bring your attention precisely to this moment. How do you feel when you are free of time?

The Seeds of Now

The Seeds of Now are preciously planted. Some may need nurturing from time to time, but I sense that they have all taken root. Words right now might only engage the mind. So, I stop writing in stillness.

"What is stillness?" asks Mastermind.

I whisper, "Stillness is immovable and yet vibrantly alive. It radiates a conscious frequency of being. Can you sense its gentleness? It is so lovingly subtle and simple. This aware sense is free of the senses."

Mastermind interjects, one more time, within time, "This is too complex. Without senses, how can I sense?"

I smile, "You cannot, Mastermind. Truly, you are the complexity. I know that it is hard to believe, but this simplicity is beyond you, since it is beyond belief. In Essence, the spaciousness of aware silence is simply speaking its rhythm as stillness, through the sacredness of life."

There is contemplative quietude and then Mastermind speaks one more time, "Well, I have to admit that this *does* sound fascinating, but I don't understand it. Maybe I should just give up for awhile."

"Yes, that's right, Mastermind. You have tried long enough. It cannot be understood. Just stop and be still. Then, wait and see."

PART 2

The Eyewitness

I used to wander ceaselessly
Looking for what was true
Hoping to find some future time
When all the light breaks through

Now I'm happy to be right here
Happy to be here now
Happy to be just here
Stopped in time somehow

In all the things I pushed away
And things I wanted near
I didn't know what I was looking for
All this time was here

Now I'm happy to be right here
Happy to be here now
Happy to be just here
Stopped in time somehow

Happy to be Here Now
From the CD "In the Heart of All Being" by Amber Terrell

Chapter One

Realize that I am

> *"You become 'transparent' to some extent to the light, the pure consciousness that emanates from this Source. You also realize that the light is not separate from who you are but constitutes your very essence."*
> ~ Eckhart Tolle

No Rain, No Rainbows

Presently, the silence of the night is in cadence with the frequency. Far in the distance, yet intimately near, an echo of the first birdsong rises through the Quiet to announce dawn. The eloquence of the song defies any qualification and thus, it remains free of imagery. It is simply the mystery of a sound of silence. There is merely perceiving, or one could say that there is true listening. The lone cry disappears into the emptiness, as a gecko quickly mimics a reply. While the world begins to awaken, the sanctuary of dawn is imbued by the symphony, with no one song distinguishable from any other.

During spring in the tropics, weather changes frequently and passionately. This morning, the sunrise is accompanied by the kinetic energy of the Kona winds. Crashing through stillness, a thunder clap near the mountain warns that rain is imminent. The azure sky along the shoreline begins to cloud, as the sun laughs and the sky cries, similar to that peculiar feeling of concurrent happiness and sadness, when the heart cracks open to merge into joy.

The ever-present atmospheric colors await the perfect ripeness and then create the splendor of a full-arch rainbow over the ocean. A faint, duplicate rainbow births into being. One of many morning walkers stops to absorb the awe-inspiring sight. As though grateful for more attention, the vivid colors intensify. The brightness forms a slight reflection upon the mirror of the ocean. No one moves, no one speaks and no one knows, as the rainbow in the sky and its pale reflection on the water radiate the potential for a full circle of color.

As the mystery begins to recede, the morning walker quietly murmurs as he saunters by, that he has never seen anything so beautiful. His eyes shine, as many eyes do on the island and he gently smiles in peaceful contemplation. Several paces away, still holding the past image, he calls over his shoulder that he wished he'd had a camera. Other oblivious exercisers continue rushing by with their eyes still to the ground, lost in the conceptual world of their goal-oriented minds.

This type of natural beauty is truly inconceivable to the mind. Mind desires beauty, but does not know what it is. In awe or by surprise, your attention is keen and the intensity of the wonderment stills thought. Freedom from conceptualized thought is the open doorway to the inner sanctum of the Heart. In pure attention, sensation flows freely without conceptualization. Free of identification and concept, the beauty resonates as simply being. From this realm of deep peace, one begins to sense the perfume of *Awake Joy*.

Nature as Teacher

Nature is revealing the Essence everywhere. Approached humbly and honorably, its pointers are extraordinary. Nature as teacher is approachable and available for everyone, while you welcome and embrace it. Simply walking in nature is a lovely movement meditation and nature resonates with the Pure Being that is. During your meditation, self-observation begins by observing externally, but you also listen to the accompanying inner dialogue and you are aware of the sensations within the body. For instance, you may be observing a tall fir, gently blowing in the wind. The inner dialogue might be something like this: "Without resistance, its branches sway in forgiveness of the wind. The trunk of the tree remains steadfast and still. Its roots are firmly rooted in the earth." When you listen to the dialogue, while observing this fir, nature is reflecting your teaching. In the above example, the lesson could be to bend and yield to life, rather than resisting. Another lesson could be to welcome kinetic life changes, while remaining still and deeply rooted within as the Heart. The flying birds, the activities of bees, the stillness of a mountain, the river that gently flows to the ocean, the still, reflecting lake are only a few of the magnificent teachers. The key is to remain fully present in the body and aware of your inner energy field of being. This assists you to be present with the appearances. Simultaneously, you are receiving the teachings in the inner dialogue and this begins leading you toward freedom.

I am not referring to mental association, where an appearance in nature elicits a memory of a past experience or the worry about a future circumstance. It is not about sitting alone in the marvel of nature, while processing "me and my story." If you are reflecting on the past grievances of ego or future desires and fears, you are not present with nature. Instead, you are in relationship with the mind-made self. Instead, be aware of how nature is acting upon the physical body and observe the feeling realization. The secret is to recognize that the mirror of nature is reflecting and resonating as the Heart.

Another example, on a mountain walk, you might discover a lone trillium, hidden in the middle of an alpine meadow. Perhaps, you would stop in honor of its dignity, beauty and aloneness. You might notice that the flower is displaying within a spacious field of silence. Be the silence within which the flower is emerging. You listen to silence, while being present with the body. What is the feeling impact? How does the silence feel within and without? Being present with the delicate trillium in this manner, you will notice a suspension of mind activity. Focus on this suspension as a gateway to the joy of being. You simply listen and remain open as the aliveness emerges. This is not a "doing." It is the exact opposite of doing. Through becoming aware of the silence and space in nature, you notice an ever-increasing expansiveness within.

You can use the senses to move deeper. For instance, in touching the alpine grass, you are aware of how the feeling acts upon you. As you eat a blueberry from the forest, you are aware of how the tasting takes effect. As you approach an alpine lake, you smell the dampness of the marsh. The fragrance of the dampness invisibly appears, as you draw nearer. You hear the alpine birds far in the distance, announcing your arrival in the wilderness and notice that the birdsong is arriving on the wings of stillness. You are aware of the feeling impact of hearing the birdsong, but you are also aware of the stillness out of which it arises. You see a fawn peacefully stepping toward the cool alpine lake to drink, as you are aware of the mystical space, within which it appears. Eventually, awareness withdraws from the object of perception to only the sensing. Awareness is one in being the listening or the seeing. By using sensing in this manner, the separation of the perceiver from the perception disappears into the oneness.

A Buddhist scholar and philosopher, Daisetz Teitaro Suzuki, who was instrumental in spreading Zen in the West, once wrote, "To point at the moon, a finger is needed, but woe to those who take the finger for the moon." Nature is only a finger and it is pointing toward you. Identification with the perceiver reinforces identification with nature. In this identification, the perceiver moves into the delusion of time and space, the requirements for conditioned thought. Then, the mind does what the dual mind does. The separate perceiver objectifies nature, categorizes and stores the perception in memory, according to its emotional relationship with the sensation and its former knowledge of the object. When this identification occurs, the perceiver no longer truly perceives, since knowledge is placed before being. The mind perceives its former concept and that is all.

Aware of Being Aware

The beauty of nature is only one medium for awakening from the dream. Virtually everywhere you go and within everything you encounter, there are pointers. Whether lovely or unpleasant, all pointers are equally valuable, since the resonation is within you at every moment. Another medium might be the fitness enthusiast in attention to perceived physical exertion. The exerciser disappears into the act of perceiving. In perceiving, the doer and the world of experience no longer exist. This merger cultivates "aware of being aware." Anyone who has been in a serious auto accident, or who has been critically close to one, has experienced time warp. In stern attention and in waiting without knowing the outcome, experience seems to move into slow motion. Beyond any notion of being able to avoid the collision, helplessness impels a deep surrender. The doer disappears in a moment of intense interest and motionless being. By totally surrendering the individual, purely perceiving comes to the forefront. If the intensity of momentary interest provokes the awareness of being aware, either awakening or detachment can occur.

Extreme sports offer another potential for awakening, since they require heightened alertness and the athlete acutely focuses on perceiving. I used to be a gymnast and later coached gymnastics, which is another excellent example that requires shrewd concentration. The attentiveness is so intense that the gymnast disappears into purely perceiving. It is not the activity that matters. No specific activity or prescribed practice can cause you to wake up from the dream. Awakening to what is eternally awake is uncaused and spontaneous. However, as concentration heightens attention, the perceiver and the perception merge into oneness. "Aware of being aware" is a signpost that you are nearing detachment to consciously pass through a portal to a deeper Truth of Being.

Peak Performance

The peak performance athlete might prompt awakening from the dream. For an athlete, it may be entering the athletic zone, which stimulates the experience of slow motion due to the intense attention. The intensity causes the falling away of the individual as it dissolves into Pure Being.

The peak performer is no longer goal oriented and in movement toward the future for some sort of compensation. For example, the goal of a runner may be to win a race. The runner is separate from the race, the act of running, as well as the goal of winning. The running is reduced to a means to an end; that of becoming a winner. The runner may necessarily ruminate in strategic thinking during the race. However, it is when a runner disappears into the running that simultaneously the goal also disappears. Without either the runner or the goal, there is purely passionate running. More likely than not, the runner becomes a winner. When there is awareness of this oneness, they may wake up from the daytime dream.

Getting lost in an activity may seem contrary to awakening or presence. However, there is a profound surrender that can occur during any activity and when it occurs, only the oneness remains. For the flutist, it is the surrender of the musician into being the playing. At the core, there is oneness. For the sufferer, it is the surrender into ardent suffering. In the eye of the storm, there is peace in oneness. When suddenly there is awareness of this oneness, they might wake up from the daytime dream.

Attentive Movement

The body is part of the content of the present moment and it is embraced by the formless Now; the only true time in the universe. Since the body always appears Now, the inner form is virtually an open window to changeless joy. When you are in conscious alignment with this inner dimension, unconditional love emerges. Lost in mind's time, the mind-made self is not aware of this window, so it feels alienated from life and believes that it was born and will therefore die. The mental illusion is that the mind-made self is living. In truth, *Life* is living and it is the formless *Being* that is Life. Being is really *Life* being and there can be no life that is separate from living. Whereas mental "living" is the limited intelligence with all of its conditions and resulting anguish, *Life* is the unconditional intelligence that is readily accessible, when you are in conscious connection with organic being.

The mind-made self is in search of joy on the mental plane. It thinks that it is moving here and there in a horizontal manner in search for something within form, while joy is formless. Can you show me joy, such as you might show me an object or thing? Awakening is a vertical drop into a formless reality that is the source of joy and unconditional love, not a horizontal movement within form. When we are still and resonate as purely being, we realize that the window is already open and that there is a cool breeze drifting through. In this, we discover that we are the joy of being.

Attentive movement is an invitation to rest as the open window, while the body moves about in the world of form. It centers us in the Now-ness of the body, the only portal to essential being. We concentrate thought in the pure attention of the inner body and therefore thought cannot be distracted. Any attentive movement will do from pouring a hot cup of tea, walking in nature, cooking dinner or simply driving your car. Eventually, attentive movement becomes a permanent meditation all day long. We live the still center point in all that we do, rather than projecting into all that is done. We recognize that it is the manner that we do and not what we are doing, that is the art of living the Awake Life.

To assist the revelation of being the still inner body, we consciously breathe and are present with the body's action. Peripherally, we are aware of our environment and use the body's senses to remain present to the

Now that is formless, instead of getting lost in mind's time. However, the primary focus is the stillness of being within us. In other words, we are aware of the immovable being, while the body moves.

Reinforcing the Practitioner

The Illuminated Rumi is a compilation of poetry, translated by Coleman Barks and illustrated by Michael Green. Below is one of the translated poems by thirteenth century ecstatic poet, Jelaluddin Rumi.

> "I have lived on the lip of insanity,
> Wanting to know reasons,
> Knocking on a door. It opens.
> I've been knocking from the inside!"

As Rumi poetically points out, you are already on the inside. When we engage in practices as a doer in order to get somewhere, we are unnecessarily knocking on the door.

Many practices for Self-discovery require a practitioner, who is doing something to become who they want in the future. The practitioner is a doer and has a goal within form that requires more time and experience. The belief is that "I am not Now" in this moment and that doing will create me in another moment. This doer is the time-based ego applying mental effort and its action arises from form, meaning from thought and desire. The practitioner's idea of striving actually protects the ego. Since form is at the forefront, the background of essential being remains hidden and unnoticed. In this manner, practices sometimes reinforce the practitioner. When you assume a practice as the doer, you are essentially agreeing to the becoming process and maintaining that you are presently separate from who you are. This type of practicing is ego's postponement strategy for the avoidance of being Now.

After all, a fragrant flower does not practice in order to bloom. It flourishes by simply being. A mountain does not practice to be a mountain, it simply is. We may practice to learn many things such as ice skating, flying an airplane or mixing colors to paint a picture. We may learn and then practice useful skills for better performance. However, for Awake Living, we surrender the doer and rest in organic being. When we are conscious of being, a deeper dimension emerges into all that we do and we enjoy our oneness with the greater life.

"I am" Meditation

While the ego acquires, Pure Being is total surrender. When we are present to being, which is natural to living, we are sensing more deeply the life that we are. We therefore sense a joyful vitality. Of course doing still appears within the field of being, however it is no longer at the forefront at a mental level. We appreciate the backdrop of the sense of "I am" through which all the forms of life appear and disappear. Form is thought, emotion and the content of the present moment, including the body. Thoughts freely come and go, while emotions rise and fall. Life experiences change and all the while, we are aware of the joyous being that is Life. Being is the only permanent factor in all imperma-nent experiences. When we do not attend the Essence of being, we are pulled into the mental realm and once again identify with form. When we consciously rest in being, we are free of form and appreciate the bliss of divine formlessness.

The portal to know that "I am" is through the body. The physical form and its sensing are always Now and a part of the present moment, so we can be attentive to our body's senses or breathing to be more present to "I am" and therefore more free of the ego. Being is *living* or we may call it consciousness. Consciousness is formlessness, as well as all form. We cannot deny that we are presently living. We just are not living "our" life, which is the ego's idea that leads to suffering. Dual in nature, "dreaming I" misperceives that it is separate from its non-dual Essence. "I am" is Pure Consciousness Being and it is inseparable from you. This Being is appearing as a myriad of forms, as it appears to be born into form and then appears to return to formlessness, all the while being consciousness.

Consciously being, we become aware of space consciousness. We are peaceful and we recognize that our actions are rising from this intelligent space. We begin appreciating the art of Awake Living, which is unified and we have no more investment in resisting form and circumstances, since Consciousness is all there is.

The "I am" Meditation is presented in Appendix II: "Practices and Meditations." I recommend this exercise every morning at rising and during periods of struggle and unrest.

Practices and Meditations

In Part IV: "The Heart" in Chapter Three: "Life is the Way," I point to being fully conscious in the present moment to receive the teachings of the Heart. Likewise in Part IV, in Chapter Four: "Awake Living," in the section "Four Roses," I share a powerful spiritual practice that is focused on the embodiment of compassion, service, gratitude and unconditional Love. Consciously living in this manner is a very effective tool to turn the ego around to discover the way of the Heart.

Finally, in Appendix II: "Practices and Meditations," I provide experiments in consciousness that concentrate attention to be more present and to facilitate the realization of "I am." They are not practices that require a practitioner. Rather, they are designed to eliminate the illusion of the doer and its body hypothesis to encounter the realization of "I am" and the Pure "I," the sublime Sky of Being. The practices include: Presence Meditation, Silent Space Meditation, Inner Silence Meditation, Testing the Body Hypothesis, Self-inquiry: Encountering Pure "I," Devotional Chanting, "I am" Meditation, Breath Control and Breath Retention.

Unity Consciousness

Before detachment, the Eyewitness rests in the pleasant sensation of simply being, "I am." "I am" is the foundation for all experience. It locks the Eyewitness into the world of form, yet it is also the open window that sets it free. When it rests as "I am," it experiences the aliveness of the present moment and this is what I term, unity consciousness. Unity consciousness is a term that I applied to best describe a direct realization. I am now aware that "unity consciousness" is defined in other teachings and philosophies. The connotation that I am applying may or may not be similar. Unity consciousness is a magnificent feeling of connectivity with all being. Even in its beauty, it is later recognized as a delusion. If you are not open to deepening, years may be spent in the splendor of this entrapment. "I am" senses the Heart of everything within its personal being. In other words, the tree is in *my* being, the mountain is in *my* being and all being is within *my* being. It superimposes "personal" being onto all form. Unity consciousness is a state, whereby the intellect aligns with its projected object, which is then experienced as unity. The feeling of connection is the result of the subject and object merging. While blissfully beautiful, it is not total submersion into the Heart. It is an experiential state and the Heart is the direct illumination making it perceivable.

Eventually the personal overlay is discarded by the Eyewitness. It recognizes the untrue quality of an "I am" that is located *everywhere* in the world of form. Who is that hiding there in the guise of "everywhere?" Yes, discovered to be nonexistent as an individual entity, the residue of ego hides everywhere, as it taints all form with its personal projection. When this is recognized, the deeper surrender is simple and immediate. "I am" surrenders to the truth of "AM," the Pure Being, as the illusion of personal being dissolves into formlessness.

If you have not yet transitioned through detachment, I point to inquiry and investigation into the Source of "I." Self-inquiry as outlined in Appendix II "Practices and Meditations" supports the realization of the true source; the reality that you truly are. Otherwise, one may simply rest as "I am," without any effort at all. Space consciousness will emerge as the space around the "I" expands. During this expansion of space, consciousness spontaneously detaches from form. One becomes *aware* of "I am" and therefore moves beyond any personal sense of "I am."

Chapter Two

The Gift of Dispassion

"The root of all desires is the one desire: to come home, to be at peace. There may be a moment in life when our compensatory activities, the accumulation of money, learning and objects, leave us feeling deeply apathetic. This can motivate us towards the search for our real nature beyond appearances. We may find ourselves asking, 'Why am I here? What is life? Who am I?' Sooner or later any intelligent person asks these questions."

~ Jean Klein

The Role of Dispassion

In the Introduction to *Awake Joy*, I shared that I had not had training in any traditions or practices before spontaneously awakening. Many expressions that I have applied were contrived to best describe what I had directly experienced. Dispassion is one of those expressions. It was a natural transition that occurred in my life story before awakening. I recognized the impermanence of all life's encounters and sensed dispassion or a loss of interest in experience altogether. Therefore, attention organically shifted inward. I am now aware that there are traditions that prescribe the practice of dispassion as a pathway to enlightenment. The dispassion of which I speak may or may not be similar. My present point is that what I refer to as dispassion was natural and not something that was self-engineered, practiced and then enforced by the ego.

Before shifting from the Eyewitness to the Pure Being, it is significant that you might confuse dispassion with malaise. Malaise is an inevitable characteristic of ego's affliction. The mind-made self chronically identifies with a sense of unease, which causes dissatisfaction to predominantly emerge. Dissatisfaction can result in melancholy or depression and can be a byproduct of ego's storytelling. Unhappiness pervades the body-mind and could be considered an addiction of the time-based ego.

Unlike malaise, dispassion is not a result of ego's internal dialogue. Dispassion is the falling away of objectivity and points toward the progressive surrender of the ego. It facilitates the surrender of the "I am the body" idea, since the senses withdraw from their objects of sensation. This offers a natural self-control, rather than a control that is contrived by the mind. If you are unaware of this passage, you may not notice ego's attempts to reinstate due to your concern that something is wrong or missing. This concern is the actual reinstatement. In the organic falling away of objectivity, the mind interprets the loss as an absence, instead of an expansion of space consciousness. This feeling of absence is a normal transition. Whereas once, you may have had a significant passion and enthusiasm for life's activities, you begin to notice a disinterest in the life story. The gift of dispassion is that attention naturally shifts, from the outer world to inner being.

Another addiction of the pseudo self is a passionate obsession with pleasurable goals. This passion addiction is often an avoidance of pain. Once ego's goal is achieved, it enjoys momentary fulfillment and it is under the delusion, that the object of passion caused the fleeting fulfillment. In truth, it was the cessation of desire. While ego vainly performs and strives, it creates tension, anxiety, nervousness and stress. Since superficial passion cannot last, when discontentment or restlessness returns, it repeats the activity in order to avoid the pain. When it tires of the repetition and recognizes the lack of lasting fulfillment, it searches for another passion. The pursuit continues without end. At last, the interest in objects is surrendered and this creates dispassion. When this feeling of absence arises, explore its nature. It may be the conscious emergence of the void of the Unknown. If so, the impression of absence and the rising dispassion are now valuable teachers.

The Passion of Presence

Eventually, dispassion allows the surfacing of true passion. Unrestrained by the confines of the ego, passionate presence is uninterrupted, blissful and stress free. It is a relaxation and globally alert. True passion is vibrantly alive, caused by nothing and in need of nothing. Reflecting upon ego's passion obsession, you might muse about your past frenzy of identified goal striving as a means to an end. What you were seeking was right here all along, except unimaginably greater. The passion of presence is powerful and its depth is unthinkable. Since the mind has never witnessed anything more powerful than itself, it bows to this passion. It is humbled in reverent, devotional silence. Its peaceful surrender into passion's fire is effortless and unequivocal. In other words, it falls in Love.

Chapter Three

The Ugly Duckling Named Mind

"Realisation is direct knowledge of the Self, i.e. it has nothing to do with the body or its senses, the mind or its thoughts — these are of relevance only to the world-appearance and the illusory ego."
~ Dennis Waite

From Conditioned to Radiant

In Hans Christian Andersen's *The Ugly Duckling*, a cygnet's identity was mistaken for a duckling. In the farmyard, he was ridiculed for being too big, too clumsy and too ugly. Since his self-image was derived through the eyes of other creatures in the farmyard, he felt humiliated and ashamed. Driven from the farmyard, the small swan lived alone in isolation, loneliness and fear. The seasons changed, as fall turned into winter and finally winter into spring as the little cygnet matured into a graceful swan. On the first day of spring, while gliding on the lake, he bowed to take a drink. For the first time, he gazed at the beauty of his true reflection. His silent response, "I never dreamed of such happiness!" Subsequently, he was recognized by like kind, who came to greet him. In splendor, he graced the lake with his elegant, s-shaped neck and feathers of dazzling whiteness.

This story emulates the plight of the ego and its fate of misidentification with name and form. Born into form as radiance, it is quickly conditioned by the mental world of form into isolation and alienation. The misidentification limits your experience to the confines of a mental-physical existence. Your eloquent nature is overlooked, through attachment to the fears and desires of the mind-made self. Nonetheless, radiance is forever present, just as the cygnet was always a swan. The ego is too big, too clumsy and too ugly, while consciously accessing only conditioned intelligence. Just as in the farmyard case of mistaken identity, the radiant mind is misconstrued and its byproduct of ultimate creativity is limited. The opportunity of this radical awakening is to compassionately and gently free the conditioned aspects of mind to swan-like Presence and it's Love at first sight.

The Nature of Conditioned Intelligence

The "me" is the knot that is obscuring the Heart, the Truth of who you really are. Of course, this obscuration is also consciousness, but the misidentification with this fictitious identity is also the source of all suffering. For Self-discovery, you untie this knot through the self-observing of the Eyewitness. The nature of conditioned intelligence is limited to your concepts, beliefs and assumptions that you have learned through past experience. Yet, you apply this past conditioning to present life. Thus, what you perceive to be your personal reality is merely your conditioning. Your lifetime is experienced as conditioned emotional reactions to conditioned actions. In other words, you are living the pseudo self's concept of past life, rather than the genuine freshness of Now.

As self-observation begins, you have a broader and more global perspective, since you are observing. You begin noticing the tendencies of the mind and you realize that in addition to conditioned thought, the nature of conditioned intelligence includes the mental images that you perceive. The body is recognized as none other than another thought that experiences the sensations of form and then the intellect interprets them from a past perspective. You realize that the emotions that you feel are none other than the emotional aspect of mind. They are directly related to your past conditioning and its separate sense of "me." From this fragmental perspective, your emotions are observed to be reactions to your mental judgments, which subsequently move through your body as sensation. Simply, you experience what you have learned and then conceptualized. Solely through memory and ensuing expectation, you re-create the past as present moment experience. You completely overlook presence, which is the only true representation of reality.

The mind-made self's trademark is lack as expressed through its idea of individuation. Lack is the destiny of conditioned intelligence. Your freedom is in your willingness to investigate the truth, through being present and becoming conscious of the programmed limitations of mental tendencies. For awhile, conditioning continues to appear. However through self-observation and detachment, you are generally no longer identified, limited or robotically controlled by the ego and its ideas. Soon, you become aware of the space around thoughts, mental images, perceptions, judgments, emotions and body. This spatial awareness embraces the entire world of experience. The catalyst for detachment and the realization of this space is the direct observation that the limited image of "I" is a pretender at best. It is only an idea, which quite stubbornly attempts to differentiate conceptually from the entire Field of undifferentiated consciousness, all the while maintaining that it is searching for wholeness and fulfillment.

It is through self-observation or what I call the Eyewitness that you become aware of ego's habituation and expose all of the trained layers of the pseudo self. In the end, the false sense of self is recognized as nothing more than another conditioned layer of thought. You are looking for life's meaning within empty concepts. All of these concepts belong to the false idea of "me." You are not the concept "me." Where does this concept point? To what does it refer? For instance, the word "rose" is totally meaningless to someone who has never seen one. They cannot associate the word with the lovely image of a beautiful bloom, with a magnificent fragrance. How can life feel purposeful, when you live within the concept of "me," while having never directly met your true "rose" nature? When you look within your sense of being, there is no "I." The word disappears into its Essence. This Essence is your liberated spirit, whose nature is joy. Intrinsically, ego must dwell in the past. It can be no more creative than the known. Abiding in the known, you are missing the mystery and the infinite potential of the unconsciousness within you.

One evening on the beach, I was absorbed in the silence of a tropical sunset, whose palette of colors was changing from moment to moment. As the sun began its sacred descent into the Pacific, a tourist started to walk by and then stopped. With his back to the present splendor, he related the problematic situations of his day in Paradise lost. Imprisoned in a self-created cage, he was oblivious to the beauty surrounding him. His blindness provided its own compensation. Meet anyone who suffers from the affliction of ego and they will swiftly begin to share their drama. The complaining has its own compensation in that the drama strengthens their separate sense of self. Storytelling makes the mind-made self feel real. Sooner or later, you tire of listening to your own stories. Finally, the anecdotes cease. In stopping, you have the promise to realize that which is beyond storybook land. *That* cannot be understood by intangible, abstract concepts in any objective sense. The beauty is that the mind cannot understand, grasp, capture, manipulate or control *That*. When this is finally acknowledged, the mind gives up. In this surrender, the Eyewitness opens to the Pure Being.

Some pathways focus on the quality or consequence of thought or action. Others deal with emotion. Still others may direct your attention to the physical form. These are all perfect, because once they are fully experienced, they can be eliminated as Essence. "I" is the first notion of all other thoughts, ideas, concepts, beliefs, emotions, images, sensations, energies and circumstances. The nature of mind includes all of these and their varying aspects appear as phenomenal experience. The Essence of who you are is transcendent of all qualifications. Your Essence is not a thing. So it is a mistake to believe that you can discover your true identity within the world of form. The non-pathway realizes the unmoving; the absolute stillness of your true nature. The mind-made self limits its reference point to the body and can only perceive from its identified point of view. It is incapable of global consciousness and this will always be so. In other words, the ego will never realize the Truth. When this is fully comprehended, the personal is finally surrendered. As awakening occurs, a deeper level of intelligence is consciously operating. It has nothing to do with a knower, the one who possesses knowledge, nor does it have anything to do with knowledge, the collection of facts, beliefs and concepts. Awake intelligence is beyond the knower and the known. It is a deeper dimension of intelligence than we normally speak of within the sphere of conditional thought.

To be free of the internal dialogue, you do not attempt to stop thinking. This is resistance and self-tyranny. The attempt to stop, which is basically more thought, is similar to constructing a dam on a river. Behind the dam, the river gains strength and force. The attempt to resist and control thought is futile. Thought is a tremendous power and its strength is increased through placing your attention on controlling it. Who is the one who is attempting control? Is it not also the thinker? Is it possible for a thinker to stop thinking? On the other hand, without the thinker, where is thought? By accepting and welcoming the internal dialogue, consciousness shifts from the content of thought, to the awareness of thought, to the awareness of the thinker and finally to itself, the Awareness.

To summarize, the external world is pointing your attention to the maze of the inner world. Initially, the inner world is almost totally obscured by compulsive thinking. The content of thought is virtually unimportant. It is meaningless to scrutinize, analyze or process the content. The internal dialogue is pointing your attention to your misidentification with the thinker. By watching, thought can no longer use you. Indeed, you may even begin to have a sense of humor about the absurdity of thought and its content. Finally, by shifting attention to the thinker, its illusion becomes clear.

Neither This nor That

Through the self-observation of the Eyewitness, you notice that "I am neither this, nor that." Anything that you might finish the sentence after "I am" is variable and impermanent. For instance in the statements,

"I am a mother" and "I am also a daughter," you eliminate "mother" and "daughter" to rest solely in "I am." Your roles change, however you remain the same. "I am" is changeless and your experience of being is consistent. To the contrary, every attribute that the mind places over being is temporary and subject to a changing experience.

During your initial inquiry, there are many relative truths that are substituted with new relative truths. You may have experienced the "ah-ha!" phenomena. As if a light goes on in your head, you discover a deeper truth. The tendency is then to crystallize the concept. Eventually, we surrender this tendency, since the moment that a realization is considered true, it is simultaneously realized as false as well. In other words, every conception is eliminated as Essence. Very simply, the Absolute cannot be a concept of the mind.

Moonbeam's Moondance

While I was in the Bay Area in California to offer satsang, I walked to the waterfront to watch the full moon rise over Berkeley Hills. I was situated on a park bench at the head of a salt-water inlet. The mountains echoed a powerful, rock-like silence. The harvest moon crept slowly over the mountains and into the secret of the night. The moon seemed suspended by a spacious quietude and reflected onto the still water. The bay provided the perfect mirror for pure reflection. Indeed, the reflection was identical to the moon. In fact, if the scene had been merely a photograph, it may have been difficult to distinguish the real, from the unreal. I marveled at the receptive coolness of the moon in contrast to the light of the sun.

Subsequently, a warm breeze rippled the surface of the water and the reflection became nothing more than undulating light. The reflection became differentiated moonbeams, creating a wonderfully animated "moondance." I suppose that one could say that the reflection became distorted. However, the "moondancing" was still a lovely reflection of the moon, just active and diversified. The appearance of the moonbeams did not mean that the moon had changed in nature, nor did it mean that the undulating light was no longer referring to the moon. Soon, the breeze withdrew into the emptiness of the night and its effect calmed the ripples. The fully integrated reflection reappeared.

And so it is with the surface ripple of thought superimposed on the depth of stillness. In identification with thought, we have the appearance of differentiation or "love-light dancing." We appear to be individuated, but we are not. The dance of identification obscures our wholeness and the diversified reflection may not seem perfect. Nonetheless, we always refer to the fullness of genuine Love. In stillness, we are a flawless reflection and we realize humanity's ultimate unity. In identification, we continue to express perfection, since Love never changes. Indeed, every microcosm is the epitome of the macrocosm of perfect Love. Neither can be realized, without the still water and the light of the sun.

Compassionately, I understand that at times, it may appear that you are alienated from sacred Love. During those times of suffering, it may be helpful to recognize that the true reflection of Love is only temporarily overshadowed by identification with compulsive thought. Perhaps, you are only experiencing the isolation of your moonbeam nature. Love is ever-present, just as the moon is still existent in full eclipse. You are here before, during and after the emotional eclipse. Conscious suffering is not comfortable, but it does have an end. No circumstance can diminish who you truly are. The separate sense of self and its consequence cannot alter the fact that you are always present as perfect Love.

Chapter Four

The Sky over the Sea of Emotion

> *"There are many stories of difficulty. Be aware that they are stories to avoid the absolute ease of being. Nothing can be easier than being nothing"*
>
> ~ Gangaji

Waves of Emotion

Awake Joy is the radiance that strings the happy and unhappy moments of the life situation together like the pearls of a necklace. In the direct realization of this radiance, the pearls dissolve into the precious freedom of conscious joy. Sensibly, inherent joy cannot be given to you, nor can it be taken away. In essence, it is who you really are. In searching for joy, you are what you are seeking and in seeking, you cannot realize your radiance.

This book is not a psychological or therapeutic guide about how to change your life story in order to be more joyful. I am suggesting that you leave the story alone for awhile and turn your attention to the storyteller. In your willingness to surrender the teller of tales, joy naturally emerges and the life story transforms to reflect that joyful transcendence. Of course, the conditioned mind does love repetition, so it is persistent. If you have ever read books to small children, perhaps you have noticed that they love reading the same stories over and over. They cherish the security of knowing the storyline and they adore the anticipation and expectation of what is already known. This is not unlike repetitive adult storylines, as we anticipate more of the same. The ego loves the known, because it is based upon it.

When you are identified with the story, you believe that outside circumstances cause your emotions to change. For example, someone does something that you either like or hate, so you feel either happy or angry. This translates to if you are happy, somebody can take it away and if you are angry, somebody else should fix it. By surrendering your true power in this manner, you helplessly ride the waves of emotion, as they endlessly rise and fall. You remain subject to their merciless push and pull. Your opportunity is to turn attention inward in self-observation and to attend to what remains pristine and untouched by emotion. At first glance, you begin realizing that your attitudes about past situations are linked to certain present emotional reactions through your conditioning. Based on past experience, this conditioning is the actual cause of your emotional storms. This is self-inflicted suffering. You cannot learn the joy of being, but you can learn how you deny this truth, through self-observation. You can observe how you drain your life force, as you willingly perpetuate negative emotion through storytelling. Meanwhile deep within, constant joy *is* without the need of any condition or circumstance. My invitation is to look deeper than the storyteller for its discovery.

The Sky of Now over the Sea

In attention to the Now-ness of the present moment, you can enjoy the sky over the sea of emotion. That is to say, you can be free of the negative impact of your memory of past pain and its reconstitution into present negative emotion. Time consciousness has its attributes and it only displays via concept. When you sense the timelessness of simply being Now, joy transpires. The time required for identified thoughts progression does not exist. Therefore, there are no thoughts to cause emotional contractions within your body. Mind can only do one thing at a time. When it is in attention, it cannot compulsively think. This is not to say that life is then listless or lackluster. In lieu of the never-ending emotional roller coaster, you experience a changeless joy, which is gleefully energizing. Free in the Sky of Now, you are free of the ego's self-created emotional drama.

Through the Eyewitness, we can discover that virtually all suffering is due to our continued relationship with the past. This view is based on ego's story-time, which is the storyline that accompanies the mental image of an incident. The result is that we mentally live our past concept in the present moment, rather than being the Now-ness of all experience. We misconstrue the Now to be a fleeting instant that is insignificantly squeezed between the past that we are trying to get over and the future that we are trying to reach. If we could examine more carefully, we would realize that the constant Now is virtually all there is. The Now is outside of time and therefore, it is the refuge of our timelessness. Timelessness is eternal. There is nothing fleeting in forever.

Through self-observation, the emotional aspect of the mind cannot use you. Instead, you become aware of your conditioning. It is usually earmarked by some sort of unease that surfaces as an emotional reaction. This is why it is unnecessary to process the past in order to be free of the past. A past fixation can only create more misery. Contrarily, when you are free of your conditioning in the present, you realize freedom from the past. Releasing your conditioned behavior is not an external action. You release it through the silent and still watching of the Eyewitness. You become conscious of your repetitive thinking and how it is linked to your emotions. Because you are observing, you no longer tend to identify with your thoughts, which source your emotional reactions. Through self-observation, you are distanced or detached from the troublesome inner dialogue. It is when you are distracted from the here and now that you identify with complicated circumstances. You are then mechanically tossed about by the waves of your past. Of course, Now always is, whether you tend to it or not. I am saying it does not really matter. In truth, you are always free and always Now. However to realize this emotional freedom, you watch your inner dialogue and are present with your emotions. Instead of resisting their push and pull, you welcome the emotions as you observe and feel them. You become conscious of your mind activity and its attempt to add intensity to emotional situations. In so doing, you become aware of the internal mechanism of perpetuation.

The Eyewitness does not change anything. I am asking you to simply watch. You will find that you are not your mind, nor the emotional aspect of mind, your emotions. This is not to deny your emotions. In fact, by fully experiencing them consciously, you realize freedom. Through uninvolved attention, you are liberated from the unconscious tendency to judge, label and categorize outer circumstances and inner feelings. Initially, your emotions are reduced to mere waves of sensation through your physical form. Subsequently, you notice that you are here before, during and after every emotion. While the sensations are impermanent, you realize that the Eyewitness is still, permanent and free. In this discovery, you are unbound in the Sky of Now.

Sailing the Storm of Conscious Suffering

Conscious suffering is being totally present with your deep emotions. When you are present with the inner body, you can sail the storm of conscious suffering, while the emotions transform into peace. If you miss your initial identification with a judgmental thought, the next signpost will be the physical sensation of a corresponding emotion. If you also miss that signpost, you begin whirling more deeply into the emotion as the mind assists the spin. This intensifies the negative emotion and it can be your teacher. If you are able to indifferently recognize the emotional takeover, you often have the opportunity to stop. Then, be still to objectively observe the feeling in the body. It is through conscious suffering that the residue of past pain dissolves. I understand that the emotional spin is uncomfortable, however there is no escape. If you resist the emotion or attempt to repress it, the emotion becomes stronger. If you act it out in the world, you are ensuring another reactionary cycle. The answer is to be present with the feeling, without further involvement, as presence transmutes the energy of contraction into the outpouring of peace.

The Inner Tides of True Compassion

Awakened compassion is not as defined by the unawake mind, such as feeling sympathy or pity for someone, who has been struck by misfortune. As formerly defined, the etymology of the word compassion came from the old French root "com," meaning "together" and from "pati," meaning "to suffer." Through this definition, compassion is suffering together in mutuality. Through awakening, compassion is redefined. While we directly recognize our mutual vulnerability in form, we concurrently rise above it. Since we have directly explored and merged with the depth of collective suffering, the unrest is transformed into the Love of the Real that embraces all form as Itself. True compassion, or perhaps co-passion, alleviates suffering all the while remaining the perfection of awakened Love. Both definitions may move us into gratuitous service however the former incentive was from suffering and relative love, while only the latter emerges as unconditional realized Love. We are then lived by this perfection as we compassionately embrace humanity, the earth and its environment.

If your suffering becomes vastly deeper than what appears to be personal, individuality as identity is being successfully surrendered and the void of collective suffering is coming to the forefront. This void is one of the most beautiful opportunities on the path of awakening and yet we tend to run from it. When we first discover this void, the collective pain may seem unbearable and dramatically magnified. In our willingness to merge with it and feel it fully, it births the inner tides of true compassion.

When form is initially relinquished, we sense an ominous emptiness. The gloomy nature of this emptiness is the result of the latent mind labeling it nothingness. To transmute this fear, we experience it. Nothingness was originally camouflaged by ego's storyline and if we are willing to investigate, we discover its true nature. Upon investigation, we become conscious of the deepest fears in the human psyche and a profound sensitivity and patience surfaces for the human condition. While being true to the perfect Love that we are, we also become deeply empathetic with others and the world of form. In this, we become compassion in action and support in any way possible. When we are awake to the present moment, the opportunities to embody this true compassion are present daily, through simple gestures of kindness, or we may contribute in a meaningful manner with world causes.

As long as the mind-made self continues to abide anywhere within its conditioning, it is subject to opposition and suffering. This opposition acts out personally within its relationships as struggle or conflict, as well as globally as war, crime, hate, greed, prejudice, terror and despair among many others. The unawake mind is simply dual in nature. In duality, the separate self conceives that there is first and foremost a separate "me" and secondly, some other separated someone that is only relatively important, when they are in context to "me." In fact, in the world of duality, if the ego conceives that there is nothing to personally gain or lose from that someone, they are not important at all. Henceforth, the "dreaming I" is indifferent. Whenever there are two, the ego has its way in opposing forces and the struggles of desire and fear continue. As long as it is identified with its separate image, the joy of oneness is beyond its reach and the Heart will continue to seem separate. Its only option is to transcend duality.

You Cannot Drown in this Ocean

In a dream one night, I was carrying the Indian sage, Papaji, in my arms. His form was so old and frail that he could not walk. I was carrying him miles across an endless bridge over an expansive ocean. However, the bridge suddenly collapsed and Papaji and I fell into the sea. He slipped from my arms and began sinking. I was frightful for the loss of Papaji's form, so I swam deeper and deeper to recapture him. When I started to embrace his slight body, underwater he hysterically laughed as bubbles flowed from his mouth and I could hear him distinctly say, "Please let go. You cannot drown in this Ocean." As I released him, his giggling form disappeared into the darkness of the ocean's depth. Today, I forward Papaji's message to you. Please let go to observe *what really is* at the depth of the sea of suffering. If suffering consumes you, then let it have you in full surrender, without further resistance. Through the Eyewitness, the ego is annihilated and gives way to the Pure Being. "Please let go. You cannot drown in this Ocean." The gift of letting go is forbearance and true compassion. It could also be the grand release of Self-discovery.

Chapter Five

Body Watch

*"The clearer you understand that on the level of
mind you can be described in negative terms only,
the quicker will you come to the end of your search
and realize that you are the limitless being."*
~ Sri Nisargadatta Maharaj

The Body Shop

The body is the manner in which Life experiences and expresses Itself
in the world of form. For this reason, the physical form is honored, but
it also has its appropriate place. The body is a thought with which the
separate self has identified and this misidentification is the source of
suffering. The inner sanctum of the body is the manner in which Life
meets Itself and it is therefore the abode of divine sacredness.

Most people are still consumed by the mental energy in the head
and actually have very little body consciousness. They may be highly
concerned with the body *image* as it pertains to its appearance in society,
but their energy is not solidly centered in the body. For this reason, it is a

good idea to get to know the body, through such activities as conscious breathing, nature walks, working out, sports and yoga, among many others. This fosters the concentration and body awareness that lead to the inner body, which is required for awakening. For these people, they believe that they *are* the body and therefore, they are attached to form. The body senses are projecting out into the world in identification with sense objects. Their *mental* attention is their point of reference and therefore their senses are somewhat dull. The first step toward wisdom is to fully inhabit the body, which requires drawing attention out of time fixation into the present moment, where the body is appearing. This requires practicing to be more present, since identification has become so chronic and the habit is so strong. Slowly, we are able to consciously inhabit the body and we notice that the senses intensify. We feel far more alive as a human *being* and we are grateful, since our world seems so much more vibrant. The field of "I am" is beginning to consciously surface, which is the Pure Being in the inner sanctum of the body. Unity consciousness arises which is a beautiful feeling of oneness with all that the body is sensing.

The second step toward wisdom is withdrawing the senses away from their objects and turning the attention toward the inner body, where it consciously rests throughout your everyday activities. We are still very much present with the world, however we no longer project the senses into the world and identify with sense objects. Instead, our attention is resting in the silent being of the inner sanctum. At first, the attention rests with pure sensing. For example, instead of projecting our eyesight onto a lovely object that we see, we rest in purely seeing. The mind is turned inward, we rest as silent being, while the senses are purely sensing and functioning as they do.

Body Watch Duality

Body observation is dual in nature, meaning that there seems to be two. There is the subject, the one observing and the object observed, in this case the body. On your next nature walk, take the opportunity to become aware of the body watch duality. We are not dealing with *what* we see, hear, touch, smell or taste. Draw the senses inward to fully experience each of the body's senses and how they intensify through attention. How does pure hearing impact the body, without attending to what you hear? Explore each of the senses in this manner. Who is aware of the sensing? Yes, the body is aware, but who is aware of the body? Is there anything deeper than the body and its sensing? Sit for awhile with your eyes closed and shift attention to the formless peace within you that is free of sensing. Do you notice that you are experiencing the peace in a dual manner? That which is observing is separate from the peace that it is observed. Can you shift to simply *being* peaceful? How does being peaceful impact the body? Is the body peaceful and at one with this peace? Now, continue your walk simply being peaceful and at one with the body.

Be aware of the body during your normal daily activities and body watch. Rest with the sensing, while you are showering, eating, breathing, meditating or simply falling asleep and waking up. Perhaps there will be many emotional sensations in the body as well. Feel them fully and then return to the body's five senses. Eventually, shift your attention to that which is aware of the body. Are you aware of the inner sanctum of peacefulness that is deeper than sensing? Those are two reference points meaning that you are in duality. The first reference point is the witness and the second reference point is the inner sanctum. In the end, shift to just being peaceful and at one with the body.

PART 3

The Pure Being

"Where i'm bound nobody knows
and i'm too far gone to take it easy
feel the grass beneath my feet as it grows
feel the wind in my hair as it blows
i've got the courage to be wrong
and the strength of a rose"

The Strength of a Rose
From the CD "Satsang" by Deva Premal and Miten
Lyrics by Miten
Copyright Prabhu Music 2000

Chapter One

Awake in the Dream

*"This recognition is freedom, freedom from that 'I,'
from that egoic pattern of striving, anxiety and suffering.
It's the release into peace and joy and wellbeing."*
~ Dasarath

The Daytime Dream

When people awaken in the dream, the reality of the world has a dream-like quality. Just as the mind dreams during the night, people are unconsciously "sleeping" in a daytime dream. Someone who awakens also discovers that the body that they once called "me" is also part of the dream. In other words, they realize that they are not the body and they are awake to the dream of form. The unconscious forms in the daytime dream appear as robotic dreamers, as though on automatic pilot. They struggle with "me and my story," which is nothing more than a dream of past memory. They vacillate in the suffering realm of cause and effect, because the entire dream is limited to conditioned existence and its conditioned reflexes. Since meaningful change cannot occur within the dream, we leave dream alone. Instead, we inquire into the nature of the formlessness within us. The Eyewitness culminates in detachment and the illusion of the dream body is finally revealed.

Free of the dream, emotion and its accompanying storyline are no longer personal. Emotions are experienced as mere sensations, within the dream body, but they do not seem to belong to anyone. They ripple through the body, much like ripples on the surface of a still lake. There is nothing personal about the sensate contractions of the body. They are similar to sound waves from loud music, as they vibrate your body when you are in attendance. Awareness shifts from the dream of form to the bliss of formless consciousness. Abidance is in impersonal being that is joyfully awake. The joy of being is now prior to the body appearance and is no longer personal. With this shift, you consciously realize that you are awake in the dream. Thoughts remain as spontaneous appearances, without a thinker to think them. They do not belong to anyone and are no longer personal. Awake in the dream is waking up to the strange, self-evident fact that you have spent your life dreaming!

Only the Light of Consciousness Is

Until you directly experience the artificial nature of the daytime dream, it is a mistake to blindly accept or reject the concept in theory. You begin observing, because you desire to know the truth for yourself. I fully understand that the daytime dream seems to be authentic. Nonetheless, after awakening in the dream, the daytime story with its problems and conflicts is no more than an ego mirage. In this case, pinching your arm to see if you are dreaming is not the remedy. Instead, you become aware of the dream through the Eyewitness and inquire into the nature of dreaming "I." Space consciousness emerges and you become aware of the space around "I." The space expands which gradually results in detachment from the dream of form.

Unlike nighttime dreams, the daytime dream appears to have continuity, giving it the appearance of reality. In other words, the story seems to be consistent from day to day. However, upon keen investigation, you begin to recognize that memory causes the appearance of continuity and therefore the appearance of reality. When you are free of past mental images, you recognize that the world is created new every moment that you become aware of it. For this reason, it is important to be free of the past in order for any meaningful change to take place.

The body and the content of the dream comprise the present moment. Who you are is the Pure Being that is aware of the Now-ness of the dream. Therefore, the Pure Being is liberated from both the body and the dream. As presence, the screen upon which the dream is cast begins revealing. As the joyful light of consciousness, you are able to distinguish all that is and only the radiant light of consciousness is. It is similar to being in a movie theater, when the movie director turns the lights on high, while the movie is still playing. You can no longer see the images on the screen. As radiance seems to dissipate and full embodiment approaches, the world exists within a new dimension of vibrant stillness. The Pure Being receives images and then they disappear without impact. Essence is all there is and this that you are is shining everywhere as every thing. In the stillness of the radiant mind, life is an extraordinary play of divine intelligence, whose sole purpose is to wake up and realize that it is awake and Self-realized.

The Mystical Dance of Life

Once consciously awake, perception is free of the aberrant shadows of illusion. All forms are mysteriously honored and enjoyed through a deeper dimension of joy. You recognize that *Awake Joy* emanates and permeates all aspects of life and is really the formless consciousness appearing as form. Life has the sense of an ecstatic Garden of Eden that is exquisitely still and silent, while forms seem to joyously dance through the sacredness. Your body and the dream are dependent upon the essential spontaneity of consciousness. "Your" being is really the unlimited Pure Being of the Heart. You are blissfully free of confinement and boundary, as well as free of space and time.

The joy of being might be revealed from time to time, when thought is suspended. However, when the mind-made self is still identified with the body, the being is peaceful but without the mystical brilliance of Pure Being that appears after detachment from form. This suspension of thought is a portal to our true nature. If thought remains suspended, *Awake Joy* emerges as a conscious reality in our lives and we are awake in the dream. However, if the suspension is momentary, we normally project onto the suspension that it was caused by something. For example, the beautiful sunset caused the feelings of joy and aliveness. The truth of the matter is that the joy of Essence is causeless and ever-present. Time stops and in an instant of no thought, a glimmer of Essence shines through. What caused the suspension is inconsequential. It could have been an awe-inspiring rainbow or the miracle of childbirth. Whenever this shock occurs and we are shaken out of time, we have the opportunity to awaken from the trance of the daytime dream. However, it is more common that the compulsive thought process resumes and it once again hides the sense of being. In this, the memory dream reappears as a mental image. The gateway to Truth is through the grace of one moment outside of time, when we are freed to enjoy the mystical dance of life.

Chapter Two

Inner Space

> *"The true value of a human being can be found in the degree to which he has attained liberation from the self."*
> ~ Albert Einstein

Objective Space

Space consciousness is the emergence of spatial awareness and it is global in nature. We appreciate an increasing attentiveness to the space that surrounds objects in the world. This focus is the conscious rising of formlessness deep within the inner body and it is a catalyst for detachment. Even while you are reading this book, while focusing on matter or content, you may be unconscious of space or silence and yet it is everywhere. We have merely been focusing on content, rather than that which surrounds it.

To the majority of the world's population, everything that is consciously perceivable is classified as real, while that which is unperceivable is mentally identified as unreal. This viewpoint relegates everything that is unconscious, uninvestigated and unrealized as unreal. We are dismissing the formless potential of space, since it is not consciously perceived. In certain respects, the advancement in today's scientific and technological communities is changing this limited viewpoint. For instance, scientists have discovered that within the atom, there is far more space than matter. Simplistically, I suppose the amount of matter might be considered to be equivalent to nothing more than a grain of sand, within the empty space of an astrodome. Scientists have shifted their attention from matter to investigate the unknown space. The problem seems to be that they are still looking for something within the space and of course finer levels of matter are then appearing. As long as they continue to look for something, the true nature of nothingness remains unrealized. Just as seekers of enlightenment, who remain non-finders, continue to look for something. On a beautiful starlit night, even the naked eye can appreciate the vastness of universal space. Yet, we dismiss the space in the assumption that it is nothing and in fact, the eye may not even notice it. The mind labels it as nothing, since there is no-thing there. What is this no-thing-ness of the unknown? What does it reflect in you?

Scientists also recognize that beyond the matter-containing universe, there is an unknown void, free of matter altogether, which is absolutely still. The scientific mind is qualifying the void as darkness. Is this really true? The true answer to the nature of the unknown vastness of space, the silence of the universe and the unknown void that lies beyond can-not be discovered externally within form. The answer is the potential of Self-discovery. This discovery does not require sophisticated scientific instruments to look for something. It requires that you stop searching and rest as still being. Totality is infinity, space, space-less-ness, matter, silence, frequency, vibration, time, eternity; the void of emptiness, the void of fullness, form and formlessness; whose womb is the absolute stillness of Pure "I." It is realized as Consciousness-Being-Bliss or *Awake Joy.* The discoveries within the scientific communities are significant, since they are opening people to the potential reality of the unknown within form. The study is truthfully pointing to the Unknown within, the Infinite "I."

All the same, it requires only a single instant outside of time to spur awakening. When this occurs, the world is virtually turned outside in. Within the time-based world, everything that was formerly viewed as real is suddenly recognized to be an illusion, which of course it is. The benefit is that the dream-like nature of the world facilitates the deeper exploration of the inner world. This inner attention allows the realization of Pure "I." This Essence is then recognized as everywhere and the world is realized as none other than the Real. Beyond space, matter and time, only the Essence is. Within space, matter and time, only the Essence is.

The Collective Consciousness

When you are in reaction to a perceived problem, the energetic negativity can physically harm you and those around you. It does not matter, whether it is mild irritation or exaggerated anger or rage. That difference is only in degree. It is the same wave length, if you will, and collectively has its physical impact on everyone and everything. If others are not conscious, they resonate with your negativity, adding more power to the collective illusion and thus escalating the insanity. More likely than not, it triggers another reaction, which in turn will become another. In this, everyone suffers.

If you have ever observed a sporting event, when rage suddenly swept through a crowd and fans swarmed the field, you have witnessed the madness of the collective. Perhaps not one single fan would have participated independently in such a manner. However, the intensity of collective negativity was such that the unconsciousness within the fans was aggravated. The energy field gained strength and soon became rage. Violence on television or in video games is another example. The unconscious are attracted and the violence begets more violence. Fixating on negativity has its impact on everyone. Imagine the impact of screenwriters, actors and directors fixating on the creation of a violent film, before they are conscious. Unconscious minds then enter the theater to fixate on the brutality and enjoy the impact of the fear. Ego's identification and desire for hostility activates hate and collectively the focus gains power. As a family illustration, when teenagers tell negative stories about their school's social environment at the dinner table, soon there are unrelated disputes among the siblings. If the parent unconsciously makes the mistake of attempting to change the energy externally while identified, the negativity is aggravated and accentuated. An aggressive or forceful external demand for change is another form of violence and fuels the present negativity. Parents have the opportunity to realize that the external is only a barometer for what is occurring within. For conscious parents, it signals that they are drifting into unconsciousness. When parents recognize that they are sinking, they can sharply realign. In Presence, they not only transmute the brooding negativity of their children, but also transmute their own past pain. With detachment, parents are able to consciously offer uninvolved attention and true compassion. This is not to say that discipline or direct communication is inappropriate or unconscious. To the contrary, a conscious and unidentified parent is quite powerfully effective. Children, especially teens, are excellent teachers for that!

Detachment from Form

When I speak of detachment, some may understand this word by a negative connotation, meaning aloofness or impassiveness. For example,
someone who acts in a detached and impersonal demeanor may be
considered by some to have a negative attribute. Before consciously
awakening, when we remove ourselves from something, it is generally
from something that we do not like. We are a "doer," who is purposefully
separating by concept. This is not the detachment of which I speak.
Detachment is a spontaneous disconnection from the world of form.
Your body appears to be in a dream world, but you are concurrently
no longer of the world. It allows a cherished feeling of connection.
Concurrent detachment and connection may sound like a contradic-
tion and it is a true paradox.

Upon detachment, the Frequency of Being may seem to deepen
or fluctuate, but the perception of variation is not true. This variation
is sourced in the residue of the intellect. We may speak of deepening,
but in reality, that which you are is already deepest and undifferentiated. You are indifferent only in the sense that you are unconditionally compassionate without preference. Mental tendencies are freed
like ancient ghosts or disembodied souls trapped in a cemetery for
eons. Detachment can occur on impulse without practice, knowledge
or teacher. It can also occur through self-observation, practices and
meditation, the skillful pointing of a teacher or the subtle rising of space
consciousness. Whenever detachment occurs, it is without warning
and its impact is profound.

To analogize the falling away of ego and the plunge into the
abyss of the collective, it is similar to being alone in a movie theater.
While the movie is running, the projector light allows you to see the

images on the film and you enjoy the movie's storyline. Absorbed in the drama, you are not aware of the act of projection onto the movie screen. Suddenly, someone turns off the movie and all of the lights in the theater. You are left alone in darkness with no experience. While ego was busy being the star of the show with its dramatic emotional overtones, it was unaware of this abyss. Identified with the images in its story, it did not realize its mental projection. Unexpectedly, detachment occurs and causes a disconnection from the images and this permanently breaks the identification. Initially, "I am the witness only" senses a darkness that is total aloneness. The gift of coming into contact with this aloneness is that we have the opportunity to face the deepest fears of the human psyche. Dying to this fear is our liberation. True compassion is born and we are able to meet the suffering of the collective and realize our oneness in deeper being. We are then truly available to compassionately love, help alleviate the suffering and selflessly serve.

The total absence of all things in the void is first registered as an existential nothingness. In other words, you sense that nothing exists. To discover the truth, you investigate deeper to see if it is as it seems. Is the absence of all things, the absence of all form, truthfully dark, or is this the intellect labeling it as nothing to promote fear? Does collective suffering have an end? Is it measurable? How deep is this formless void? Are you willing to investigate the depth of the collective ego and its human emotions? For example collective human sadness is immense, but if you are willing to merge with it without resistance, an actual appreciation arises for the beauty of its absolute emptiness. This merger transmutes the sadness into true compassion. Always inquire into a negative emotion, "Is there anything deeper?" and keep following it to its deepest root.

Before detachment, you may unconsciously fear this darkness, so you avoid looking beneath the surface of life, yet the void lurks. Deep in the psyche, the more refined layers of illusion persist. The only way to know the true nature of the void is to directly encounter it. The unwillingness to experience sadness, or any other negative emotion, gives free reign to the runaway imagination of the ego. Unconsciously, you may have tried to repress the fear of this void. Fortunately, you cannot escape the shadow. It follows you everywhere begging for exposure to the light. The gift of awakening is to finally explore the reality of this shadow. As you open to welcome suffering, forbearance appears, since we no longer fear suffering. You begin to transmute enduring tendencies, as well as the illusion of collective suffering.

Stunned out of Body

Detachment may initially cause some physical disorientation. For some, it might also be accompanied by a sense of fragmentation. One moment, your center point is the inner body, the next it is completely stunned out of body and into a deeper realm that is free of the body altogether. Ramana Maharshi once jokingly shared that the impact of awakening on the body is similar to trying to fit an elephant into a grass hut.

When detachment occurs, the witness is totally free of the body and we begin realizing that body action is happening by itself. It is simple to observe that breathing occurs without our involvement. We know that bodily functions, such as digestion or the heartbeat, do not require our involvement. With keen attention, we recognize that every action that the body takes is simply happening by itself. For example, perhaps you are resting and suddenly the body gets up to get a drink of water. As presence, you can appreciate that the action begins by itself. Action does not require a mental decision. A millisecond after the movement begins; the mind owns and possesses it. For instance, "I am thirsty and I am going to get a glass of water." This is the mind's interpretation of the action and not the mental decision to act. The body moves into action before thought. Functioning is always primary, whereas thought is always slower and secondary.

While consciousness seems to assume the limitation of the body, it is not true. It remains unaffected by any boundary whatsoever. After detachment, you move deeper than the field of bodily experience. Consciousness is free of the body, whereas the body *is* consciousness. The body is utterly dependent upon the spontaneity of consciousness. Before detachment occurs, attention is solidly within the inner body and subsequently, "the inside of the inside," and the body now appears within you. Attention then shifts to see who is watching and Awareness becomes aware of itself. Those are two reference points, which means duality persists. The delusion of the split is due to the illusion of the witness.

After detachment, the physical form seems lighter and more spacious. This sense of expansion increases your awareness of any denseness from accumulated past pain that is being stored in the body. For some, there can be discomfort of which they were not previously aware. Alternatively, these symptoms could also be pointing to a fear of deeper surrender. Pain demands attention and therefore, it is an effective distraction from letting go of the body. In other words, if there is pain, it anchors you to form. When you detach from form, you are free of the discomfort, even if it persists for the dream body. In any case, it is important that you fully inhabit the body throughout the awakening process. It is grounding, it increases alertness, it helps release the residue of past pain and it supports the comfortable transformation of the body.

If the body has pain, you can direct attention into any physical denseness, rather than away from it. How does pain feel in the body? Is there a core to the pain? How does the *inside* of the pain feel? With your eyes closed, can you feel a boundary to the pain? Is there contraction around the denseness? Is it possible to expand the energy, rather than contract around it? Is the contraction resistance to expansion? Relax more deeply to be present with what is in acceptance, without labeling it. Remain attentive and observant, without a need to change. It is through welcoming and accepting, instead of resisting, that you may enjoy release. You soon recognize that if you are aware of the pain, you are also free of it. "I am the body" idea, transforms into "I am not the body." Ultimately, "I am the body" and "I am not the body" are both false concepts; however the shift moves you deeper into consciousness.

Visions and Psychic Powers

After detachment, you may experience extraordinary phenomena. Visions and psychic powers may appear within the world of experience. As with all experience, you are here before, during and after the incident. Although mystical and perhaps fascinating, phenomena are impermanent and exist within the realm of subtle form. You cannot find your-Self within visions or psychic powers, so do not be seduced by their superficial magic. This seduction is ego calling you back to limitation. Visions and psychic powers are meaningless distractions. You do not need to mentally evaluate the meaning of a vision or a certain power, since it is only an appearance. Essence is transcendent of mind-created visions, psychic powers and all other phenomena that appear in the field of experience. It is beyond demonstration and the one and only power. Discover who you really are and then visions or psychic powers either appear or they do not. Their presence or absence is basically meaningless.

Chocolate Cake

Awake Joy is a guide to the Heart and is designed to be your companion throughout your journey to Self-discovery. Therefore, it emphasizes significant transitions to encourage deeper awareness, rather than residing in any sense of arrival. If you can decipher from this section your current reference point, you will have at hand the awareness that leads to a deeper surrender that will ultimately happen anyway! The awareness of your current reference point means that you are already *beyond* it, since you are *aware* of the point. The direction is always toward that which is aware. A point of reference is a general indicator to move beyond.

As an example of using a reference point, I might ask someone for directions to a certain address. If my search address is nearby, that person might first ask, if I know where the Post Office is. I am not looking for the Post Office, but the reference point is helpful in orienting. Likewise, I am not directing you to the reference points below. They are meant for general orientation. You might first review in more depth certain sections of this book and then proceed by investigating for yourself within that area.

The analogy that I am going to apply is a multi-layered chocolate cake. I further expand the nature of the bottom layers in Part I: The Dream and Part II: The Eyewitness. I develop the top layers in Part III: The Pure Being and Part IV: The Heart. Each dimension is parallel to the one above it and all exist simultaneously.

The body reference point is the bottom layer. I am the time-based ego and I am identified with the dream of form. I am not aware that I am dreaming and that my world is the mental image that I am projecting. My attention is on you and I am not conscious that this focus is to primarily enhance or protect myself. My identity is my body and I am unconscious of being. This layer is the battlefield of conflict and I am the sufferer. I am also an illusion. As the ego-body, I believe that this is the only dimension and I am not conscious of the layers above me.

The Eyewitness reference point is the next layer and I am the self-observer. The Eyewitness is a study of me, my form and my interactions with my world; the study of the false. I am still the ego, but I am progressing toward freedom of this state of consciousness. I continue to look out at you, but I am primarily interested in "me" for the broader purpose of self-understanding. I study my personal consciousness as the subject of my world. "I am the body" idea is at the forefront and I predominantly attend my inner objects of thought, physical sensation, mental images and emotions. I am becoming conscious of my personal suffering and how it perpetuates.

The "I am" reference point is a layer that is beyond "you and me." I am conscious of my being and I am attending the space around my objects in the world, as well as my inner space beyond my thoughts, mental images, emotions and body. My abode is the inner body, but I am not yet free of form. I enjoy a beautiful feeling of connectivity with all being and appreciate oneness within the world of experience. In unity consciousness, you and I are one and I am at one with all that I experience. I sometimes get lost in time fixation and therefore, I still identify with thoughts, but I can release them when I become aware of it.

Detachment is not a reference point, but it is a marker. It is a thin layer of icing that is applied before adding the next cake layer. Formlessness dynamically disconnects from the body and I am no longer identified with the idea of "me." I am now consciously awake to the dream of form and the world is unreal. This shift is a universal transition and allows the bliss of *Awake Joy* to vibrantly emerge. The icing bestows the mystical phenomena that are commonly associated with awakening.

"I am the witness only" reference point is formlessness and I have no form. My being has transitioned to the Pure Being. I am the primal sense of being-consciousness-bliss and the substratum of form. I have surrendered conflict and I am now the playground of peace. I release subtle layers of the intellect and transmute the illusion of collective suffering. If thoughts are present, I have no sense that they speak in any real way and thus personal suffering is impossible. I am also conscious that the layers below me are unreal. I am not aware that duality persists. In other words, two subtle reference points endure. I am not conscious that I am still a reference point and that I will be eliminated.

"Pure I" has no reference point whatsoever and I am the final layer of our cake. "Pure I" is Self-realization and the fulfillment of non-duality. Not one word that I could say would be true.

The Heart is full embodiment and I am Awake Life. The bad news is that we are not going to *take* this cake and eat it. The good news is that we are going to *give* it all away by serving it. The chocolate cake is not ready to selflessly serve without the fudge frosting! The frosting is the art of Awake Living.

The purpose of this chart of reference points is to assist your current perception. Once perceived, it is not calling for mental interpretation.

Instead, we release the perception to open to the essential Essence to which they point. Interpretation will lead to analysis and theorization, which will conceal and sabotage the purpose of the charting. Throughout all of these transitions, the Pure Awareness that I am never changes. Whether I seem to take on form or not, in every case, I am the Eternal Now that is Life. I no longer differentiate between any of my dimensions and I am fully integrated as the Totality.

Chapter Three

Impermanence and Permanence

"Life, the universe, time and space appear in
Awareness! That Awareness is here, now."
~ Isaac Shapiro

The Nature of Impermanence

When you surrender all that is impermanent, what remains is who you are. Every "thing" in the perceivable world and even very subtle layers of formlessness are subject to the law of impermanence. This means that everything that appears will eventually disappear. Forms come and they go. If you are searching for something unchanging and lasting within impermanence, you will suffer. It is self-evident that impermanence cannot contain permanence. No-thing is permanent.

When you observe object consciousness, you recognize that everything is in variation. People, places and things appear and then disappear. Situations, ideas and circumstances, all change. When this becomes perfectly clear, your attention shifts to observe dreaming "I." You notice that thoughts, emotions and the body are in constant movement. The layers of unrest within the inner world become very subtle indeed. To discern the most refined levels of modification within the void, you remain in still attention. Only permanence is able to discern impermanence and only permanence is able to *realize* permanence. The culmination of discernment within formlessness is Self-realization.

As an example of searching for permanence within object consciousness, you might search for happiness in your career. However, you can recognize that careers are in constant variation. Therefore, stable happiness cannot be realized through your profession, regardless of its positive characteristics. There will always be periods of unhappiness. The situations, colleagues and responsibilities change. If you continue to maintain the belief that a career should not make you unhappy, you will change careers and try again. Bewildered, when happiness continues to elude you, perhaps you begin searching within some other changing situation. For instance, you might try to find stable happiness within relationships and this is also destined to fail. Since people and circumstances change, relative happiness will cycle to unhappiness sooner or later. While relationships may provide many moments of lovely, relative happiness, it is intermingled with unhappiness. In fact, stable unhappiness is just as impossible as stable happiness, since it is subject to the law of impermanence. On the other hand, joy is inherent in both. When they merge into oneness and the transcendental is realized, joy transpires. Transcendental joy is free of duality and therefore free of vacillation. Your birthright is changeless joy, regardless of any circumstance. When you give up striving for joy, through objects, people and circumstances, it signals that you are closer to realizing the joy that you are.

Discernment

If *eternal* joy truly exists, it surely must already be here now and its nature must be permanence. To uncover changeless joy, it requires the discernment and surrender of all that is changing. By analogy, if you were to imagine that you were identified with being a wave on the surface of the ocean, you would notice that the wave is temporary and impermanent. The wave moves as it comes and goes. By discriminating movement, your identification with being a wave would be realized as false. By surrendering change, your realization would bring you closer to who you really are. In your willingness to *not* know who you are, you would remain open and watchful for change. Continuing our analogy, perhaps you would then observe that you were really the ocean, until you felt the push and pull of the tides. By relinquishing the tides, you would dissolve into the stillness of the ocean's depth. The nuances of the intellect become evermore subtle and perhaps even the depth of the ocean would seem to come and go, to be impermanent and therefore you would further surrender. Perhaps you would recognize that the essence of both ocean and wave seems to be water, so you would diffuse into being water. However, even water changes form, so it would be recognized as impermanent as you would realize vapor. All the while, you rest as presence, which is the permanence of still Awareness.

And so it is with awakening. By being present and unchanging, you are able to discern that which changes. When changing is noticed, the surrender spontaneously occurs. Then, you remain still to discern deeper change and this continuing openness is essential. For instance, when you rest as pure being, the mind eventually rests. Because of this, some may confuse the absence of thought, as having attained enlightenment.

Self-realization is more than a blank state of no thought, so we remain open for deeper discrimination. This discernment is the permanence of the living Essence within you.

In quietude, you observe the noisy and the noiseless. In clarity, you observe lucidity and confusion. In peace, you observe harmony and conflict. As freedom, you observe the coming and going of that which is open or free and that which is closed or contained. Resting as Totality, you observe unity and separation. Forms spontaneously rise and fall in permanence. You are able to discern fluctuation and instability in the temporary due to your steadfast timelessness. It is through the discernment of the ever-changing that you realize absolute security. It is remarkable to surprisingly discover security in the Heart of insecurity.

Just as the sun does not know darkness, Essence does not know non-Essence. Fully integrated, you realize all apparent diversification, as none other than Essence. You are the eternal Essence that encompasses all form and formlessness. Your timeless permanence supports all impermanence. You originate the rise and fall of the present moment and while time cannot embrace timelessness, your timelessness does embrace the movement of time.

Chapter Four

Surrender, Presence and Welcoming

*"Awake. Be the witness of your thoughts. You are
what observes, not what you observe. There is
no way to happiness, happiness is the way."*
~ Buddha

Four Intensities of Surrender

Whenever you experience longing in your life, its root is yearning for love's conscious completion. It is through surrender that you are released into the joy of this divine sweetness. On your inner journey, you will pass through four intensities of surrender: unconditional, unequivocal, vigilant and transcendental. All are realized through presence. As your surrender deepens, the more refined layers of assumption are shed. If it is your truest wish to realize love's freedom, you are irresistible in your yearning, total surrender, unrestrained devotion, innocent inquiry and steady vigilance.

Bhagavan Sri Ramana Maharshi's Beloved Guru was the Holy Mountain Arunachala. In *Arunachala Pancharatnam*, Ramana poetically writes of the surrender required for Self-realization, "By your grace alone my heart lotus blossoms, O Arunachala. Then I will be immersed in the vastness of your bliss." Another beautiful example of surrender was when Jesus said, "Let Thy will be done." When you recognize that freedom is greater than "me" and beyond the reference point of the subject-witness, pure transcendental surrender is causelessly realized.

For purposes of discussion in this chapter, I am distinguishing unconditional and unequivocal surrender. I will also differentiate vigilant and transcendental surrender.

Resistance is the Ego

The ego judges circumstances from its fractional viewpoint of fear that displays as either inferiority or arrogance. Its effect flows into life as programmed reaction. As a pawn to life, the ego experiences either painful repression or aching reaction. For the mind-made self, it is one powerless reflex after another. Based on past belief, it is caught in a web of cause and effect. The result is an ongoing struggle for power and security. It maintains the belief that happiness is an outcome of outward striving, acquisition and attainment. From its memorized past, it projects future desires, all the while on guard to defend and protect its treasured point of view and objects of desire. Residing in either future hope or past fear, it sabotages the here and now, as it hungers for personal gratification.

The opportunity of awakening is to recognize that you are free of ego's push and pull cycles. If you begin observing your inner world, you are able to discern the effect of this vacillation. You recognize that your identification with the image of me, the ego's fearful judgments and tainted future hopes are actually the cause of suffering. In other words, the suffering is self-inflicted. Once you become aware of the cycles, you can then recognize that the one who is aware is already free. By focusing on that awareness, instead of the content of the mind, the ego and its inherent negativity eventually evaporate. Our preoccupation with time is defeated, our avoidance of timelessness is terminated and our misidentification with the false sense of "me" is finished.

Unconditional Surrender

Unconditional surrender is surrendering to the life situation. It is a surface surrender that deepens into the wisdom of Self-realization. Unconditional surrender is a willingness to allow each moment in the life situation to be as it is, meaning that you unconditionally accept life. Throughout your lifetime, experiences have conditioned you. Gain and loss have an emotional impact and that becomes your mental point of view. The result is that the past lives on in you and dulls the freshness of the present moment. It is overshadowed by your mind activity, much like clouds hide the sun. To become aware of this mind activity, you can become more aware of the physical sensation of resistance. The body will begin to feel uneasy and tense. When you sense these contractions, you can then shift attention to your inner dialogue. That dialogue is a result of the past and the manner in which the past perpetuates. By simply observing the mental conditioning, you become more liberated from the ego and a deeper surrender is the automatic result.

By allowing the moment, ego begins losing its power and mechanical, reactionary nature. Life breaks the ego much like a horse trainer breaks a wild stallion. Ego usually has an idea of how it wants life to be and then tries to make life conform to its individual desire. The result is more suffering for you and others. This is pointless, since life is as it is anyway. Whenever you have a sense of unease, you can be certain that "mastermind ego" is still up to bat and ready to swing its idea of what life should be. To be free, you unconditionally surrender to one tiny segment called the present moment. You basically no longer resist the flow of life as it appears moment to moment.

Unconditional surrender is not just an outer phenomenon, but inner as well. By this I mean, it is more than an outward appearance of acceptance and meanwhile the mental activity indicates otherwise. For instance, we may communicate to someone that we are not upset, but the truth of the matter is that we are brooding in mental negativity. Our outward appearance looks normal, maybe even loving, but inside we have a battlefield. Instead of acting out externally, we act out within. The situation is already past, but we continue to feel tense, since we are pondering how it should have been or maybe strategizing some sort of future revenge. Meanwhile, we are overlooking the joy of present living. I am not suggesting that we should try to change the inner dialogue, since that is only resisting our resistance. Instead, our still attention transmutes the negativity into true compassion. We can even welcome our inner resistance and feel the inner impact of that release, which is an opening into the expansiveness of joy. Free of resistance, life is graceful and we experience an ease in living. The river of life is then peacefully rambling through us. A surrendered life will carry us to the joy of the Ocean, if we would just let go.

Resistance seems unique to the human being. Nature provides many examples of yielding to life, rather than resisting. In a tropical storm, a palm tree yields to the wind and then regains its graceful sway. A river yields to its gravitational force as it descends a mountain to enter the ocean. Winter yields to spring, just as the ocean yields to the tides. A bear surrenders to hibernation, rather than weathering the snows. An eagle soars in the sky and yields to the wind. Daytime gracefully surrenders to the intimacy of the night. Thought free, nature meets life as it is and never slips into time.

Unequivocal Surrender

Unequivocal surrender is broader in nature, such as when we invite a higher power to live our lives and then remain true to that surrender. We surrender our anger, our fears, our anxieties, our desires and our enlightenment to the one who knows the way. The surrender is unequivocal in that you are not only releasing the destiny of your life story, but also the separate sense of self. When we let go of these contracted burdens, we enjoy a gentle lightness. This relaxing surrender is a powerful transformer of negative energy and then we are free for more genuine living.

Has struggling with life been successful? Has striving provided fulfillment? It is somewhat strange that as soon as we give up, joy rushes in. Through unequivocal surrender, we are creatively animated in right action that is free of thought, decision, judgment and worry. We relinquish all illusion of control, manipulation and choice. Basically, we rest in "not knowing" and every life experience becomes a mysterious adventure.

When Surrender is the Ego

When the "me" vanishes along with its desires and fears, we realize that there has never been anyone here to surrender. Resistance and surrender can be two sides of the same ego-coin. On the edge, between resistance and surrender, there is awareness. Within this awareness, the illusions of both resistance and personal surrender appear. Who could be separate from Totality to surrender and to whom? What could be separate from Totality to surrender? Who is that hiding there in the name of surrender? Once again, we find the ego. As soon as we begin to surrender resistance, the ego discreetly moves toward surrender. When we can become aware of the movement, we can stop and rest as the still awareness. In stillness, there is no doer to resist and no doer to practice surrender.

Vigilant Surrender

Vigilant surrender is the willingness to attend the sacred flame of love in our Heart, rather than observing our thoughts. We are present to life, but attention is resting primarily inward. The correct posture is one of *being* the sacred flame, rather than objectifying it as a separate thing as in duality. Regardless of the life circumstance, we are faithful to being the glowing light. This vigilance has an inner feeling of objectless worship, adoration and devotion. The attention prevents the confusion of our conditioned existence from invading our inner space. We "protect" our flame, just as we would protect a candle from the wind. We keep our inner space open, free and clear. In this manner, we are then able to recognize the slightest movement to contract and the burning attention transmutes mental tendencies into the precious fuel for true love. In adoration, we devote to being love's light, instead of the phenomenal display called life experience. If we deny this light, we will suddenly find ourselves in the world again and we get lost in the struggle. We merely shift attention back to being the open flame.

In vigilant surrender, we welcome the opposition of others as a rising teacher for inner space.

Transcendental Surrender

Transcendental surrender is our opportunity for the most profound surrender. It is the surrender of the world of form and sacred formlessness. As Jesus of Nazareth spoke, "Love the Lord thy God, with all thy heart, with all thy soul and with thy entire mind." In other words, *everything* is surrendered and it dynamically happens without warning. For transcendental surrender, we have unconditionally, unequivocally and vigilantly surrendered and we are able to rest as still, open awareness. Transcendental surrender is the final yielding of the witness, when the witness is recognized as a mere point in consciousness. Duality plunges into the splendor of the non-dual Pure "I." Nothing can promote transcendental surrender. Preceding this ultimate surrender, you may sense that you are resting in what I call "the waiting place."

Glimpses of Truth

Through the intensities of surrender, we are frequently blessed with glimpses of the radiance and then it seems to disappear. Thus, a pointless search begins to reclaim it. In this, ego is successful and its idea of becoming reinstates. The sole illusion of loss is caused by the idea that "you" attained. That is the reappearance of "me" and so its shadow causes the impression of loss and obstruction. If we then try to recapture bliss, the obstruction persists. The ego's tendency is to try to capture the most significant moment of a lifetime and then to conceptualize the glimpse as a personal experience. In other words, the ego tries to possess it. If you begin the effort to reclaim the glimpse, you are agreeing that you are separate. Instead, simply be still. The illusion of the one who is glimpsing, attaining, losing and reclaiming will dissolve. You cannot lose or attain the bliss of Essence; you can only *be* Essence. Rather than lamentation of imaginary loss and frustration over a futile search, the clear answer is to be the unprotected, still being that you are.

The Grace of Welcoming

Welcoming is the attitude of surrendered living. A sense of gratitude emerges for every life expression. We welcome life as the amazing mystery that it genuinely is. Our inner posture is one of receptivity, while life reflects the wonder. The world of experience is displayed through a dimension of quiet stillness, while the mystical forms appear and disappear. Just as a gracious hostess is home to greet her most honored guests, Grace receives her tired children and frees them to enjoy creation.

Chapter Five

The Waiting Place

> *"And if you rest here, you will see that everything is happening by itself; that thoughts and actions come by themselves. Everything is moving along just fine, without you pretending to control everything. And then you rest in this moment. You can dive deeply, unceasingly into this moment and disappear into the sweet nectar of silence"*
> ~ Kip Mazuy, Bliss Music

I am the Witness Only

Detachment allows the space of the Pure Being to emerge in its purity. Purity is not the purity that relates to its opposite, namely impurity. It is a Field of simplicity, clarity and basic goodness; it has no related opposite. Purity is free of the pure-impure cycle and yet lovingly allows the illusion of good and bad to appear, within the Field as form. I embrace the world and the universe, while I shine forth. In form, I am gentle and humble, but also powerful in sharpness and clarity. Purity offers loving purity, since all images are the Pure Consciousness that I am. Nothing is excluded from this omnipresent, omniscient and omnipotent Self.

Love naturally speaks love unto itself and I exhibit relentless devotion, with doubt resolved. I am true compassion and the radiant mind is pure, harmonious and creative. Life is holy and sanctified.

As the witness only, I taste the real and the unreal; meaning the dream world of form and the being-consciousness-bliss of no-thought Essence. I am a bridge between two worlds. Some may set up camp on my bridge with a sense of having arrived, because of my blissful nature. Instead, I continue to allow the ground beneath my feet to fall out. Crossing over is my purpose and I am the portal to formlessness. I do not notice that I am still maintaining my role as a subject, not a personal subject of course, but a formless subject. The point in consciousness that I am prevents integration and full embodiment. I am not conscious that my very reference point is still maintaining duality. When I become aware that I am witnessing the Heart as an object, my point of reference will be eliminated.

"I am the witness only" recognizes that the external and internal worlds of the body are mental constructs. What appeared to be the inner objects of thought, emotion and form are now realized as object consciousness. All objects are false as Self-identity, whether conceived to be outside or inside and this includes the objectified "I." The witness realizes that consciousness is prior to the image of "I." This reference point is outside the troublesome thought process, free of the ego image and free of form. In the unwavering resolution that true identity is not sourced within *any* aspect of form, detachment surrenders the Eyewitness and opens into the Pure Being of formlessness; the witnessing consciousness. Thoughts freely appear and disappear in this space. Without identification with the thinker, thoughts are only intangible forms floating by like a river through awareness. Detached and unidentified thought may still have momentum, however the witness is free of attachment to thought, including the "I" thought and liberated from the limited reference point of the body. Once established as the witness only, you are no longer fooled by the ego and its ravenous desire for time. Tranquility of mind comes to the forefront and the stillness of being expands. Thought ceases its outward projection and attention rests deeply inward.

Attention basically shifts from the "I am" of unity consciousness that is located everywhere as the oneness in the world of form to the opposite point of reference, nowhere. It may be difficult to discern that nowhere is still a point of reference and it points to the formless reference point of the witness. It observes an existential nothingness as the idea of non-existence appears. The void is a total absence of all form and the exploration of formlessness begins. After detachment, the witness is free of dreaming "I," free of the body and free of anything personal.

The root of consciousness is the source of collective suffering. To expose this root, the light of consciousness is shone into every dark corner of the collective nothingness. This collective includes humanity's fear of death, total extinction and non-existence. With the powerful impact of detachment, there can most definitely be Self-realization. However, if the root of consciousness has not been transmuted, these deepest collective fears will likely surface for transformation. "I am the witness only" is as far as the intellect can go. Anything deeper is beyond cognition and the witness no longer has the impression that only the conscious is real.

Satsang or Awake Essence

The term "satsang" is an eastern term and is most frequently translated as "in association with Truth." In other words, you are sitting in a gathering with "the awakened." In English, we do not really have an expression that is an accurate equivalent. In fact, this popular translation is slightly off point. At first glance, the difference may seem subtle, but in reality, the difference is problematic to Self-discovery. If you conceptualize that you are seated with the awakened, you are focused on the teacher. The teacher is none other than your-Self and if you are looking at the teacher as something other than you are, or more than you are, you cannot *be* who you truly are. The translation is dual in nature and therefore serves as an obscuration. Satsang is *being* Truth, not "in association with Truth."

I frequently call a meditative meeting Awake Essence. We rest in the feeling realization of "I am" from the Eyewitness viewpoint or simply "AM" from the Pure Being viewpoint. In Awake Essence, live words emerge as a current of stillness, however words do not even need to be spoken. Upon leaving satsang, consistent presence to inner being is required. It is a mistake to conceptualize that Awake Essence ends at the conclusion of satsang. Essence is the divine Truth that you are and therefore is always with you. Throughout our daytime activities, we live in a movement meditation as still being, until purely being is consciously permanent.

Control, Forbearance and Selfless Service

In the waiting place, there is no place to go and nothing to do, so life is quite simple and calm. The sense of waiting is free of anticipation and expectation. There is no one to wait and nothing to wait for and yet a sense of waiting prevails. The life experience that appears is always a mysterious surprise. We remain watchful and seem to be spontaneously animated in right action. The surrendered life is free of control, hiding and pretending. The notion of choice and free will has been surrendered. We are no longer shy about being awake and are able to openly share the joy. We are not discreetly hiding that we are fulfilled or pretending that the awakened life should remain unspoken. We no longer feel slightly apologetic for our discovery, while being with others, since all is recognized as consciousness. On the other hand, we are not demonstrating that "we" know something that "they" do not and have no investment in changing anyone. We simply have a deep knowing that everything is perfectly happening the way that it is. The natural curiosity of others arises by our manner of living. They will ask you for pointers, when they are ready to hear. We may find that Truth is clearly speaking through us and we are also listening. We no longer confuse a conditioned reality with the Truth. The pure expression of Truth has no holdback, discrimination or manipulation, in either action or word. The waiting place is one of joyful equanimity.

In this waiting place, forbearance appears. We have discovered the depth of true compassion and we delicately welcome suffering with patience and without resistance. We are tender with ourselves and peaceful with others. Our total acceptance is true Love, while knowing that life is the way. We have an understanding that the deeper value of someone's agony is to diminish the ego and is ultimately its final destruction. We are able to be fully present and spacious with others in their painful experience, without getting caught up in their personal storytelling. We recognize that pain is in movement and therefore will come and go, while we remain the ever-present Essence that we are. Our compassionate presence is merciful and tolerant of the human being and its vulnerable state in form. The deep love that emerges is free of restraint and allows serenity and tranquility to be present in every circumstance. Our inner space remains effortlessly open and this deeper surrender is the catalyst to realize non-duality. We recognize that we are the benevolent awareness, through which the appearance of suffering passes, while we remain still as the witness only. Forbearance is a signpost that we are in the closing stages of the apparent affliction of consciousness and near the conclusion of the perception of human suffering.

Compassionate kindness and selfless service also emerge, since we are a willing and an available instrument of consciousness. We joyfully give without the idea of getting something and the giving is not personal, it is selfless. Joy is the natural outpouring of that which we have realized, which is the effortless action of overflowing love. Fundamentally, we simply rest as the sweet emanation of silent service that voluntarily stirs love into action.

For discovery, *Awake Joy* is beyond the dream world, but in the end, this Essence is embodied. Joy, love and bliss are as natural to the human being as breathing and we are beginning to live the Awake Life. We transcend the appearance of the unreal and then embrace the earth and its creation as none other than the Essence that we are. Free of the dual, unawake mind, kindness and tolerance are innate in conscious living. Self-discovery offers the foundation for a selfless society that peacefully serves and shares with one another. Through awakening, love seems to be asking for a more conscious expansion and a deeper life of compassionate being.

I Doubt It!

Finally in the waiting place, we encounter "I doubt it!" At this point of the book, I can only point to that first single-lettered word at the beginning of the quote. It is clearly mind activity and no more than a persistent echo of ego. Doubt is harmless unless you attend to it. Remain present to wisdom, instead of the confusion of the mind. This clarity is the resolution of all doubt and you are "Kissed by the Angel of Peace."

"Kissed by the Angel of Peace"
May 10, 1998

Today is your birth-day, so I place at your feet a lotus.
Wiggle your toes and feel the softness of the petals.
Look at the radiance that surrounds you, the perfect reflection of you.
Inhale the perfume of your sweetness.
With a sigh, release the fragrance to the universe and just be.
Open your mind and see that the open Heart is listening.
It listens to your loving, living bouquet.

Today is your birth-day, so I cradle you with soft feathered wings.
They are the wings of compassion, nurturance and true love.
Every feather is enchanted.
They blanket you in harmony and peace.
For just one moment, enjoy the reverie of freedom.

Today is your birth-day, so I blow to your lips one bliss kiss.
Look into this angel's eyes and surrender into sacredness.
Gaze past the nakedness of open and surrendered eyes.
Be stunned by Grace. Every thought in the universe is humbled.
You are the Rapture of the Infinite!
Your heartbeat is the very pulse of Presence.
The window is already open.
Can you feel the Breeze?

Today is your birth-day;
It is time to stop pretending!
Let's disappear into the splendor.
One breath breathes this inexplicable *Living Joy*.
Be joy, since you *are* joy.
Be peace, since *you* are the Angel of Peace.
Emanate the fragrance of the lotus.
Embrace with the wings of true love.
Imagine! Your birth heralds the birth of humanity.

Today, your birth-day, it begins with you!

PART 4

The Heart

"Our spirited Self doesn't need to be understood any more than the smile of a child, the beauty of a flower or the splendor of a sunset. The nature of such encounters is fulfillment and the intellect cannot serve to enhance such moments. In fact, if you bring thinking to a sunset, you are likely to miss its sacredness and beauty altogether. Without thinking, you are taken in. With thinking, you are seeking entrance."

Free Spirit: A Guide to Enlightened Being
~ Excerpt by Sundance Burke

Chapter One

The New Dawn

Tripping Over Joy

What is the difference
Between your experience of Existence
And that of a saint?

The saint knows
That the spiritual path
Is a sublime chess game with God

And that the Beloved
Has just made such a Fantastic Move

That the saint is now continually
Tripping over Joy
And bursting out in Laughter
And saying, "I Surrender!"

Whereas, my dear,
I am afraid you still think

You have a thousand serious moves.

By Hafiz as translated by Daniel Ladinsky
I Heard God Laughing

When you are finished with your thousand serious moves and ready to trip over joy, it is time to meet the Divine. Prepare to meet your final Lover and let your garments of the mind fall to the floor, for they are no longer in fashion. Your intimate encounter is just before dawn.

Chasing Life

In our youth, we loved physical activity simply because it was fun. We ran during recess, played games on the playground and went swimming. Perhaps as young adults, we believed that working out would make us more attractive to reach our relatively modest goal of happiness. Then later, when we saw our parents getting a little older, we approached our lifestyle in a slightly different manner. Perhaps we became more watchful of the foods we ate, the stress in our lives and exercised for better health or longevity. All of these mind-body activities can be helpful, fun and fascinating. However, who is chasing life? Is Life chasing life? Only the thought-based self could be in pursuit. Does it not make sense that the perfect opportunity to realize *Life* would be while we are *living?* Are we awake to the fact that who we really are was never born and will never die? Eckhart Tolle once shared that the opposite of life is not death. Birth is the opposite of death, while life has no opposite.

Why Are You Here?

Most people still equate their identity with their physical form. This concept casts a fearful shadow, since it is assumed that when the body dies, "I" die too. We may fear that we will no longer exist. Our chance is to stop our avoidance strategies. Death of form is not going to go away just because we ignore it, for there is no escape. Each day, it seems that the body marches closer to its inevitable death. Moreover, it is pointless to analyze death, since death's partner is the mental voice causing the fear. Through belief, we can face death through a leap of faith and theorize that it leads to a life everlasting. Even so, mental belief will not extinguish the fear. Instead, we can look directly into this haunting image in the mind to inquire what it is that we are running from and helplessly moving toward. To make this fear conscious, we invite it into attention.

The fear of death is caused by our misidentification with the physical form, its limitation and impermanence. This is similar to the mistake of yesteryear, when it was believed that the world was flat. Everyone thought that if they sailed on the sea to the horizon, they would drop off to their death. In fact, the horizon was so feared that no one ventured near. That is, until someone actually faced the fear, sailed into the unknown and discovered a world that no one even knew existed. We are free to superstitiously avoid the venture toward death's horizon, but we are also free to explore the unknown to discover the truth. The presence of Eternal Life does not require the death of the mental body and the result of this inquiry extinguishes all fear. The reality of the continuity of Life then requires no leap in faith.

Before Benjamin Franklin discovered electricity in the atmosphere, no one knew that it existed. In today's world, it seems almost inconceivable that there was actually a time when people lived without it. Today, we take it for granted and are dependent upon it. Awakening to the truth of Self-discovery is different, in that the discovery is not a "thing," such as electricity. So, we may find ourselves too skeptical to take a proclamation of eternal wakefulness too seriously, since the discovery is who we are beyond our physical form. Some may simply be too doubtful that we could honestly not know who we are or whether we could actually realize Eternal Life, while *living*. Flowering into this timeless dimension is similar to Franklin's discovery, in that electricity was invisible, but present. However, our eternal Reality remains invisible and yet its frequency is here nonetheless. Beyond our form, we are the Now-ness of infinite Life. This Essence is forever present and is neither limited, nor time bound, nor confined to the physical form. It has no dependence whatsoever, including the mental body. The body is no more than an intangible thought form that appears in consciousness and is only perceivable due to the Self-illuminating nature of the Heart.

Since Life cannot be shown to us, such as electricity through a wire to a light bulb, it requires our present inquiry. Our culture has created a certain lassitude of waiting for the answers to be handed to us. However, awakening to eternity requires our direct exploration. Whether we choose to investigate or not, consciousness is awakening within us anyway. It is similar to a forest fire that spreads on its own accord. It is a silent fire and affects everyone, whether we are conscious of it or not. It is our only true Reality. If we investigate beyond body consciousness, we discover that we are not a temporary, finite fleck within this Field. The brilliance of the discovery outshines all fear and the illusion of death is no longer an enigma.

How deep is your desire to realize this living Truth? In the end, you ask, "Why am I here?" and "Who am I?" What is your lifetime purpose that rests in the core of your Being?

Love, Serve and Remember
From the CD "Remembrance" by John Astin

"Why have you come to earth?
Do you remember ... Why have you taken birth?
Why have you come ... To love, serve and remember."

Divine Longing and Fearing Death

All desire is based on discontentment. Simply, the ego desires what it does not have. The superficial desires seem to be endless. As soon as one is satisfied, another arises in the mind. The resurfacing discontentment points to something deeper. When we live in identification with ego, it generates a feeling of separation. Through steady inquiry into the abyss of this separation, we may eventually find that the deepest longing is to know God. Since we have accepted the assumption that we are our physical form, we may believe that we have to die for this meeting. The mysterious dichotomy then seems to be that our deepest longing ends up being what we fear most. This dilemma could only prove to be confusing and confusion always points to the mind. In the collective consciousness, the quandary of this dichotomy could only manifest in the world as turmoil. Instead of attending to mind's confusion, we expose the fear of death and make it conscious. With this willingness, we discover the duplicity of death, the truth of Eternal Life and embody fulfillment. Otherwise, we spend a lifetime longing for a divine reunion, which can never be known in any objective manner anyway and concurrently fearing what is required for that meeting.

To meet death's deception, the witness innocently follows the divine longing into total absence, where it meets the fear of death. In the Heart of this fear, we realize that we are free of death's image. We psychologically die and realize that there is no death. In this, we appreciate the consummation of a lifetime of yearning and the mirage of fear is finished. We realize that we are free of all desire and live fearlessly. Death is ego's figment of imagination. The trio of the witness, the ego's identification with the body and the fear of death walk hand in hand. They are banished in the Heart of darkness. You are Life and you have only to say, as Hafiz wrote, "Yes! I surrender!"

The Valley of the Shadow of Death

After a mystical experience in 1654, Blaise Pascal wrote, "There is a God shaped vacuum in the heart of every man which cannot be filled by any created thing." This void of nothingness is our salvation, when we are willing to walk into "the valley of the shadow of death" to explore. The void is qualified as the absence of everything, so we meet collective darkness. This absence is the Eternal Life's open doorway. We meet the collective fears of isolation, abandonment, hopelessness, helplessness and death. The root of humanity's cumulative fear is the fear of this void. As we have discussed, duality requires two reference points that disappear simultaneously to realize non-duality. In this disappearance, Life is realized as the Heart.

In the valley, whatever fear arises, the witness is that "wave length." If the witness meets hopelessness, it becomes hopelessness and inquires,

"Is there anything deeper?" In the willingness to be this cumulative fear, the fear is exposed to the Light of Consciousness. The witness descends into the valley of aloneness and the Love that the witness is releases all illusion. Every manifestation of collective pain becomes the witness and the pain cannot withstand the Love of the merger. Luckily, in total darkness, it is easier to notice a tiny pinpoint of light. True compassion then midwives others as they face passion's fire, with patience, tolerance and mercy.

The Concept of God

This section is not saying that God does not exist, nor is it suggesting that you are God. Self-discovery requires that we surrender our abstract beliefs, so that we directly discover the Truth. The last belief to be recognized is the *concept* of God. In other words, we are maintaining an empty idea, rather than realizing our Being as the Heart of God. The abstraction of God arises with "dreaming I" and both disappear simultaneously with the witness. The witness is surrendered, when it is realized that the dimension of the Heart is being witnessed in a dual manner.

I am That!

The purpose of the self-observing Eyewitness is to lead to detachment from thought, emotion and form, including the "I" thought. The four-fold purpose of "the witness only" is to realize the oneness in the bliss of being, to recognize that Awareness is aware of Itself, to explore sacred formlessness and subsequently the delusion of the collective void. When objectification is perceived by the witness, one could say that the emptiness of the void turns inside out into overwhelming fullness, which embodies the Totality as "I am That!" The gift of full embodiment is the integration of all form as the Essence. The Essence is undifferentiated *Awake Joy* with no point of reference whatsoever. As the intensity dissipates, only the calm, rock-like joy remains and you are the bliss of all form as none other than Essence. As Jesus of Nazareth spoke, "The Kingdom of Heaven is inside you and it is outside you. Split a piece of wood and I am there. Lift up the stone and there you will find me."

"Silent Mystery in the Heart of Night"
May 19, 1998

She pauses in the late afternoon, the Beloved's breath whispers through her hair. She inhales the breeze of silent joy, this invisible gift of Life. Spring exudes the scent of lilac, while the earth offers other fragrances of the Garden. Together, we birth the birdsong and echo the chime. Twilight intimately greets the sunset and her skin still carries the warmth of day. Enjoying the woman's wonderment, the Beloved asks, "Who are you?"

"I am Purity and Innocence," she radiates. The fragrance of white orange blossom trickles forth. Grace pulses the symphony of color as the Garden delights: healing green, dancing fuchsia, laughing yellow with trumpets of purple, smiling faces of cream, a circle of blue that features eyes of lavender. "Beloved, how do we describe this beauty?"

"Purity, I am simply the quiet Mystery that is breathing, listening, seeing; the sensing and the perceiving. My Heart beats eternally. Look inside and be the Inside of the inside. Who are you?"

She breathlessly whispers, "I am the crimson cloud that reflects the blush of my cheeks. I am the joy of embodiment, the Heart of the silent mind. I am the overwhelming gratitude of Grace. Yes, gaze through these eyes. You are so mysteriously charming!"

She feels graced, as she drifts into infinite darkness. The body dissolves into the empty void of all mankind. "Is there anything deeper?" One is absolutely quiet ... no mind to dream, no-thing, no one; only sacredness and the Rapture of the night. A humming Frequency quickens. "Who are you?"

"I am the Rapture in the Heart of darkness, the salvation of all mankind." Without notion, the blazing Light reveals no night, as pure "AM" restores the radiant gift of "I am."

The morning is kissed with everlasting openness. She moves through the day as the open Blaze *is*. She is the still center of clear blue, full emptiness. She embraces every eye and emanates this unseen Joy, while silently inviting, "Who are you? Would you like to disappear? When will you look? Let's share this holy communion of Life!"

Inside, she coyly smiles the knowingness of the loveliest of nights, in the secret Garden with the silent Mystery in the Heart of night.

Chapter Two

Spontaneous Awakening

The Awakening Story

Spontaneous awakening appeared over twenty years ago and I would like to briefly share that story with you. However, I emphasize that these events occurred in my life situation, whereas Self-discovery is not within the realm of the individual and its story. The Heart concerns the greater Life underneath the life circumstance. No *individual* attains enlightenment, since Self-discovery is the culmination of everything personal. For this reason, it is also the end of the illusion of ignorance and suffering. Truly, enlightenment and ignorance are conceptual counterparts, whereas their Essence is transcendent of both. In realization of this Essence, joy naturally outpours into the life situation and embodies as true fulfillment.

Until 1986, my life as a public school educator, an operator of aerobics studios and a mother was as "normal" as any other life story. While growing up, I had profound spiritual experiences, but I had never meditated, or been a seeker of Truth. In fact, I had never heard of Truth or the concept of awakening. My friends were not on this path and I had never heard someone speak the word "enlightenment." After awakening, I did not even know what subject to reference in my search for intellectual understanding. One thing was evident; no one knew what I was talking about, including spiritual teachers, psychologists, psychiatrists, physicians and clergy. In reply, they would often sit silently with eyebrows raised, finally offering well intended, but meaningless, direction.

In my professional life situation, I was highly energized by my aerobics business. I was physically fit and experienced ecstatic joy during teaching. While practicing the roles of ballerina, gymnast, cheerleader and aerobics instructor, my father had told me that my body was like a finely tuned sports car. I recognize now that all of those activities facilitated the opening into the natural inner attention and body awareness required for awakening.

One of the reasons that I loved my business was the opportunity that it offered to support people. For example, I once asked an aerobics student why she came to class every day, even though she could not participate, since she had broken her knee cap. As tears brimmed in her eyes, she shared that it was because she experienced in class, the same energetic ecstasy that she had experienced during the birth of her first child.

In my familial life story, I deeply cherished being a mother. My daughters accompanied me to the aerobics studio and initially participated in the Moms and Babes class, then Tiny Tots and finally the children's programs. In the end, they came to help with the work. I treasured their relationship with their grandparents and my husband was a successful attorney. You can imagine his and my parents' sense of dismay, when I suddenly told them that I had discovered a new dimension. I shared this *unbelievably* good news with my friends, never considering for a moment that it was *unbelievable*. Eventually, when they lovingly shared their doubts concerning my mental stability, I reassured them that this had nothing to do with the mind, even as I peered into their doubtful faces. In my exhilaration, I even shared with a few of my aerobics students, the miraculous discovery that they were not really the body and that I was not even Katie. So, what was I to do with a business named Body by Katie? Well, it caught fire and literally burned.

The awakening occurred while I was teaching my aerobics class. I went into an "athletic zone" and everything went into slow motion. This was not an unusual experience, however this time I was stunned by a subtle synergy that caused me to become intensely alert. It seemed like I was sensing some ethereal, new dimension. Suddenly, the zone opened and I was falling through a numinous and vast spaciousness. I suppose that it was somewhat similar to my surgical experience as a preschooler. I fluttered on the ceiling of the operating room, while looking down at the doctors around my tiny body on the operating table, until I sensed that my body was alright. Then, I was gleefully swept into a vortex of darkness, just like *Alice in Wonderland*. Free of the body, I rode different colors of lightening rods, the last of which was purple. It was the most vivid and the longest in duration. Pure white light then appeared. I disappeared into the light and light was all that existed, until I lost all awareness. Upon regaining body consciousness, that small child sensed that she had actually died.

In the aerobics room that day, the fall into the vast spaciousness was absolutely quiet, exquisite and vibrantly alive. Although I have tried to write about the gap in experience, I have no memory of what then occurred. When I became aware again, the class of aerobics students seemed far away and somehow above me and I was no longer sourced in the body. Distantly, my form was still enthralled in the movement of aerobics. I felt an overwhelming joy and I sensed that something very sacred was occurring. It was oddly clear that I was not the body and I was completely detached from form, emotion and thought. "Katie" had shattered. I felt an unconditional love and bliss that were beyond my understanding. I was established in a palpable, new Frequency of Being and everything around me seemed exquisitely pristine, as though I was sensing for the first time.

When I returned home from the studio, I laid down in the meadow beside my home to sense the frequency of the sky. I turned to look by my right shoulder and noticed a lone meadow flower gently bobbing in the breeze. I watched in wonderment as a honey bee landed to feed on the nectar of the flower's center. The flower gently bowed and acquiesced in synchronized balance. I marveled at the simplicity and harmony.

I noticed that the frequency quickened while walking among trees, so I frequently sat in the still solitude of Bridle Trails State Park adjacent to my home. In the distance, the space around the Cascade Mountains seemed massive and appeared to be calling me. This was the end of my life as I had known it and the beginning of a profound inward journey.

By accident, I discovered that the frequency quickened at Mount Rainier, so I went there frequently to sit. Slowly, I became aware that this frequency of being was emanating through everyone and everything. In fact, it was the very Essence of my true nature. Detached, unidentified thought continued to have some momentum; however it had no real significance and did not seem personal. To seek distraction from the Frequency, the mind subsequently contrived a volume of suffering circumstances, within the life situation. I became a victim of identity theft, which was troublesome for the dreamer within the dream; however it was also perversely amusing, in relation to the discovery that I had never been "Katie." More seriously, my home and my belongings were destroyed. My daughter was in a critical car accident. There were many other serious endings and complex life circumstances. That is, until forbearance appeared. No longer successful in negative distraction, the mind contrived the paradoxical beauty of visions and other powerful phenomena. While initially mystifying, eventually a sense of humor arose and I wondered what the mind would think up next.

Sundance, Gangaji and Eckhart

In 1988, I met Sundance Burke, who was an attorney that I hired to settle my aerobics studio fire loss. Today, he is my husband, frequent teaching partner and author of *Free Spirit: A Guide to Enlightened Being*. Sundance awakened in 1982. I feel blessed for the destiny of this meeting and for the extraordinary life circumstances that followed.

A friend gave Sundance an audio cassette by an Indian sage named Sri H.W.L. Poonjaji, also endearingly referred to as Papaji. He said that Papaji had an American student named Gangaji. In 1994, we went to see Gangaji at a public meeting in British Columbia, Canada. It was the first time that I had heard someone speak, what I had realized to be true. It was a stunning confirmation and the complete resolution of any remaining doubt. First in silence and then verbally, she introduced Sri Bhagavan Ramana Maharshi, who was Papaji's teacher and who is universally distinguished as one of the greatest sages of the twentieth century. During the meeting, I heard Gangaji suggest to someone to move into their suffering. I had already realized the illusion of personal suffering and that it was none other than the void of humanity's collective suffering. However, during the exploration of this emptiness, I was left with the impression that it was of immeasurable depth. I noted the possibility that the perceived nature of this collective might likewise be an illusion.

One morning, I woke up and my body was rigid. I could not move my joints and muscles. After months of this immobility, I explored the absolute depth of the void. I entered what I now term "the valley of the shadow of death." I recognized the subtle separation of the *concept* of God and of awareness being vigilant unto *That*. Without effort, the reference point of the witnessing consciousness was obliterated and all dissolved into full integration. I consciously realized that *I am That!* as passionate joy surged forth. After three months, the intensity dissipated into a calm and steadfast *Awake Joy,* of which I am the very Essence. My body began a gradual release. Self-discovery was not really of this world and I was in silent service.

A friend from Canada introduced me to Eckhart Tolle, the author of the international bestseller, *The Power of Now.* In meeting Eckhart, it was Beloved at first sight. I was invited to assist on tour and in his offices in Canada, which was my first step back into worldly functioning.

Subsequently, there was what I call a gradual, full embodiment of the Heart. This joyful embodiment is the art of Awake Living.

"Enigmatic"
November 26, 2004

I am not two, nor am I one.
I am the unqualified Totality that offers them.
I am neither place, nor universality.
I am the unknown Infinite that supports them.

I am not time, nor am I space.
I am the eternal Now that allows them.
I am neither the body, nor the world.
I am the limitless Pure Being that lives them.

I am not changeable, nor am I reliable.
I am the permanent Absolute that yields them.
I am neither moving, nor motionless.
I am the steadfast Beyond that sustains them.

I am not emptiness, nor am I fullness.
I am the pure Heart that nourishes them.
I am the True, the only Reality.
I am the Essence that is Awake Joy.

> And only *This* I am.
> You too are only *This!*

You are Pure Consciousness, the Self-Realized Bliss.
You are the Two, as well as the One.
You are Place, as well as Universality.
You are Time, as well as Space.

You are Changeable, as well as Reliable.
You are the Body, as well as the World
You are Moving, as well as Motionless.
You are Emptiness, as well as Fullness.
You are the Essence that is Awake Joy.

> You are *This* I am.
> I am *This* I am.
> And only *This* is!

Chapter Three

Life is the Way

The Teachings of the Heart

My awakening occurred without spiritual practice or previous knowledge of awakening and enlightenment. To my good fortune, I could not find anyone who knew what I was talking about. I say fortunate, since my only option was to live Heart's revelations and to perceive its pointers. I was amazed to consistently perceive them everywhere; the mystical space surrounded everything and the Frequency was the profound backdrop. Nowadays, people have heard of awakening and there are so many brilliant teachers and lovely books that are radiantly sharing. In addition, I would like to call your attention to the consistent pointers in day to day living. I share the following experiences as metaphors to demonstrate the normal progression over a lifetime toward realizing Life's purpose; awakening to your true nature.

I would like to once again point out that you are already That which you are seeking. It is impossible to deny that you already *are*. You *are* when you are living daily life, you *are* when you are sleeping and you *are* when you are dreaming. Moreover, you are *aware* that you are. However, you have become conditioned by untrue ideas. So for Self-discovery, we remove the false ideas of the mind that cast a veil over the Truth that is ever-present. Through still attention, Awareness realizes all that is untrue and it is surrendered. When all that is false is eliminated, what remains is who you are.

Life is not a means to an end. It is more than endless projects with deadlines to get you somewhere, so that you can finally be here. This is equally true during one's awakening. Life is *living* and you are its very purpose. When you are receptive to the Heart's teachings, the pointers are always there. Life is always leading toward the Heart. It can only reveal its reality, when you are fully present. Whether before awakening or thereafter, *life is the way.*

With hindsight, I now see that all of my life experiences were leading me to the Heart's way of living and in the end, to fully embody the Awake Life. Yes, our true teacher is within us always, but it is also displaying through everyday life. *Life is the way*, when we are present. For example, I was a ballerina, cheerleader, gymnast and aerobics instructor. Through happenstance alone, this increased my mental concentration and inner body awareness that led to spontaneous awakening. Furthermore, the Heart's way was making my mind-body known in an extremely focused manner. Accordingly, I realized that I could not find my-Self within its action. Eventually, this guided to the discovery that I was not my body at all.

When I perceived that my partner was at fault for problems in our romantic relationship that only I was experiencing, my partner's mother gave me the name of a psychologist. I knew nothing about the rational-emotive therapy that the psychologist employed, nor was I really interested at that time. I just wanted my partner to change. This therapy pointed to watching thought and how it interplayed with emotion. Once engaged in observing, I was quite fascinated. Although, my problem seemed to be that when I intuitively looked inside, there were no thoughts of which I was conscious. Hence, the therapist taught me to use thought like a tool in order to get angry. While I was a pro at sadness, anger was foreign, except for normal squabbles with my siblings while growing up. Anger always took me by surprise, when I encountered it in others and I could never quite grasp it.

This did not mean that I then conversed with my mate in an angry manner, but I could better communicate, what I perceived I needed. Because I was present with my communication to him, I clearly saw that it was mere thought in action. Thought was not inside at all, but outside at some mental level and it was a tool to get somewhere. With the understanding that thought's role was one of utility; I did not take it so seriously and I was able to release the need for my mate to change. I was able to be more present with my partner and also more present with my problematic thinking. I was looking out and looking in as one sight. The deeper value of this encounter was that I directly experienced the impact of my thoughts on my emotions and it provided a more conscious self-understanding. *Living* was the practice field and it naturally provided the perfect format to live deeper.

During that same time frame, Helen Reddy was one of my favorite recording artists. I loved "The Last Blues Song," because even though the words were sad, the music itself was very upbeat and joyful. One day after teaching school, I turned the volume on high and began dancing in the living room by myself. Soon, trickles of tears were streaming down my cheeks, as I continued my dance. Although I had played and sang along with the song dozens of times before, I suddenly heard her words, "I think that I am getting high, on feeling low." I stopped dancing and turned the music off. I realized that not only during my dance, but also in my life, if I were to be honest, I was actually "getting high on feeling low." While this was not my last blues song, it was definitely a valuable signpost to recognizing my game. Eventually, I surrendered the game and lost interest in its lack of authenticity. The natural outcome was that self-observation was a forerunner to awakening. My point is that life is always mirroring your answer. It consistently provides the perfect circumstances, whether the mind and its judgment call them ideal or not. The truth of *living* can only reveal itself, if you are in conscious attendance.

In the last chapter, I told a story of my surgical experience as a preschooler, so I will only share briefly now that I rose out of my body and my awareness floated on the ceiling, while looking down at my tiny form. I then fell through darkness until light was all that existed and I lost all awareness. This was clearly a preparation for "I am not the body" that occurred so many years later, when consciousness detached from my body during spontaneous awakening.

Similarly, as a primary school student, I went with my best friend, Sherry, to her summer Bible School camp. We were given the opportunity to invite Jesus into our hearts. At the moment of my invitation, I experienced that Jesus fell into my heart and from that moment seemed to live my life as my friend. This prepared the way for the unequivocal surrender that was required for awakening and the direct recognition that there was something greater than "me." Furthermore, this presence was inside my heart.

When we were only ten, Sherry died. The night after her surgery, her mother noticed that she was silently sitting on a stool in the kitchen and gazing out the window for a very long time. Her mother finally asked if something was wrong, since she was normally so animated. Sherry told her mother that she was going to die that night and she did. As her best friend, I saw Sherry's form after the death and it was perfectly clear to me that the body was not Sherry. While I was deeply saddened by her death and felt an absence that plagued me throughout my adult life until my awakening, I never sensed that who she was had died in any real way. She was *living* as a loving presence in my heart, only no longer available to be my playmate. Even my own surgical experience as a preschooler offered support for the truth of Sherry's passage. The understanding is that Life *is*, whether with form or without.

What is more, the truth of Sherry's surrender of form prepared me for the surrender of mine in awakening. It also lighted the pathway for my acceptance of the shattering of the ego named "Katie." In spontaneous awakening, I was stunned out of my body, not in the sense of an astral projection; in fact it was the direct opposite. Instead of rising out of the body, I disappeared so deeply within it that the body disappeared. This was disconcerting in light of the fact that I had a successful business named Body by Katie and in an instant I had neither body, nor Katie!

Likewise in high school, I went on a camping trip with my church's youth group. In the tent after bedtime, the youth minister's wife was in a lengthy discussion with someone who was an atheist. For what seemed like hours, she was encouraging the girl to change and she was adamantly resistant. I finally felt that I could not take the push and pull of the conversation any longer and dropped my face into my pillow and thought, "Leave her alone!" Suddenly, a numinous silence filled the tent and everyone sat up in extreme attention to the stillness. Light glowed in the tent and I remember turning to see if perhaps the headlights of a car were causing the illumination. I experienced the light as somehow a part of the mystical silence, although its presence seemed separate from us. When the light and profound stillness dissipated, without a further word, the atheistic girl had been transformed into a believer or indeed, more than a conceptual believer. The stillness and Peace provided a direct knowing for all of us of a Reality that no longer required a leap of faith. In the morning, the youth minister shared with the other campers that we had experienced a miracle; the very presence of God and it very quickly became a story of the mind. Only upon spontaneous awakening did I recognize that the camping experience was a gratuitous glimpse of my true nature. I just did not realize it as such.

None of the anecdotal stories that I have shared with you required knowledge or planning for their natural passage, any more than the natural maturing process of growing up. As children or as adults, we learn many valuable things, but we do not need to practice *living*. Living is the pathway to awakening and it is a natural transitioning for the human being. *Life is the way.*

Since I shared the story of "me and my awakening" in the last chapter, I am not going to repeat it here, other than to share that upon reflection, it was the natural culmination of a lifetime of experience, itself being a non-experience. I have no sense of having arrived any-where. After all, I am *living*. I just no longer have any place to go, other than being the Mystery of Awake Life as it now appears. I do not have a feeling that I am unique or for that matter peculiar. Awake living is just normal now. With all of its idiosyncrasies and what the mind might call its imperfections, it is perfection. What used to seem normal to the mind's idea was really quite limited and not normal at all by any means. Just like waking up in the morning or turning thirty years old or forty, through maturing wisdom, we naturally awaken to the Essence of the human being and embody this Truth.

Finally, I would like to convey that usually the conditioned intelligence has its idea of what it thinks that enlightenment is supposed to look like, when in fact it only knows the known. People who have not yet awakened may want awakening as a means to some ego-end. Since this is the destruction of our childhood toy named ego that we have carried into adulthood, no one gets anywhere. Everything is simply taken and subsequently, all is given. Yet, True You remains the only enduring Reality.

If you have had a glimpse of Essence, it is dynamic in contrast to what you think is your existence. Any initial glimpse is often attributed as having a direct cause by the time-based mind. It may be attributed to aerobics, a meditation practice or yoga, a glance or physical touch from a realized teacher as transmission, but the truth of the matter is that the timeless Essence of who you are is already awake within you now. The dust of the mind and ever more subtle layers of the intellect are merely brushed away to reveal it. Nothing can cause what already is. Every self-observation, glimpse, awakening, detachment, enlightenment, being born or dying, or for that matter getting a drink of water or taking a walk is spontaneous and uncaused. When the ego hears these words, it may conceive that this is the perfect chance to act out its adolescent ideas. Because of its opportunistic manner, it may profess no personal responsibility for any action. While this is ultimately true, this personal intent only seals the fate of its destruction. The result is that it is ensuring another suffering circumstance, through the ego's idea of control and manipulation. This is good, since this destruction will eventually lead to the final annihilation of the ego, when unequivocal surrender is the only option. In the depth of this surrender, a sacred Life is realized.

While reading this chapter, perhaps you feel that your life has not had the types of encounters that I just shared with you. I have been meeting with people for many years and I can honestly assure you that true pointers are always present. Upon reflection, you will see that every peak experience, every low experience and indeed every average moment are pointers to the fact that you are *living*. Your life is never trivial, when you are present to *living* and open to its mystery. *Life is the way.*

"The Mystical Sky"
Friends of the Heart April 2007

Can you sense the Changeless as the white clouds drift across the pale blue sky? This morning, do you hear the inaudible Silence of the red-breasted cardinal, while its song is outpouring? Are you aware of the unfathomable Perfection of the brilliant colors of the rainbow? Is not the Infinity of space truly awe-inspiring as the stars twinkle in the midnight sky?

Do you feel the Harmony within as the sun sets over the Pacific or the Mystery of the full moon over Lanai? Are you distinguishing the Stillness, when a blue-tipped butterfly suspends in imperceptible space?

Well, close your eyes for a moment. Yes, there are many thoughts and corresponding feelings. Do you notice that they are all either about or in relationship with "you?" Have you discovered yet the blissful joy beneath happy and sad, when you stop talking story?

Now, just rest as "I am" and stop at that ... nothing more. Still with eyes closed, back away a little. Are you missing the space around "I," the sublime sky of being? Are you able to discern that this sky is still within the field of experience? Are you any less, if you resonate solely as "am," this beautiful feeling of connectivity?

Evermore subtly, perhaps still unconscious, does any reference point whatsoever remain? Not a personal reference point of course, but *any?*

Is there anything deeper than even the slightest movement ... or stillness ... of inner experience?

Upon Self-discovery, open your eyes. Let it all settle in, so to speak. Can you be in this world, while not being of it? Is there any difference between That which is within and That which appears to be manifesting everywhere?

Are you fully integrated and embodied as the non-dual Heart? As True Sky, are you now experiencing the sky, the cardinal, the starlit night, the rainbow, the sunset and the moon as the purest joy of True You?

Chapter Four

Roses for Awake Living

The Way of the Heart

Blessings appear in every aspect of our lives, when the human being is consciously fulfilled. This One Life then emerges as the art of Awake Living. We live the natural way of the Heart in a profoundly human manner that is globally undivided. This unity is in cooperation with the human species, the living earth, its vital environment and in harmony with the welfare of its creatures. The quality in which we live is not one of personal choice that is mentally selected as a right way based upon moral virtues, but rather the organic outcome of the total surrender to the Heart. The Spirit is fully integrated as we contemplate our relationships, workplace, investments, health, schools and politics. It is not that living becomes a spiritual practice, but rather our multi-diversity is appreciated as a symphony of Love in action. We have assimilated a balance in our daily lives that includes the spiritual in every encounter as it appears. We are virtually a free instrument of the Heart and selflessly serve Its way. Awake Living is conscious that we are being lived for the good of the whole.

Four Roses

The roses are limitless in this abundant Garden. Today, I offer you four; they are compassion, service, gratitude and Love. Each has been chosen for its fragrance, brilliance and foremost for its power in turning the "mind's life" around, to the open way of the Heart.

The pink rose of true compassion is a gift of basic goodness to alleviate the suffering of others. Compassion flows from the emptiness and its cultivation purifies the mind. You allow your heart to be touched and are deeply empathetic with human conditions, while compassion stirs you to right action. Compassion is the work of mercy and fosters basic kindness. You are *the whole* and embrace the creatures of the earth and protect the natural beauty of nature. This compassion includes a feeling of the joy that appears in others' lives with equal warmth and gratitude. You care for life for what *Life is* and for what *you are*.

The white rose is a gift of purity and innocence in the silence of serving others, the earth and its creatures. It is silent in that the service is selfless and humble, free of personal interest or outcome. With no motive in service, the quality is far beyond the mind and its ideas.

The fuchsia rose is one of gratitude for the Life that appears each moment. You express gratitude to others, the greater Life for its abundance, the earth for its trees, the sea for its gifts, other living creatures and insects for their service to Life and the weeds that you pull as you smell the earth to grow your rose garden. In the end, gratitude overflows the Heart of Life until a grateful Heart is all there is.

The red rose of unconditional Love is the greatest, since virtually every petal contains all the others and indeed, the entire Garden of Awake Living. This gift appreciates Life's truest passion for loving with patience, humility, forgiveness and emotional maturity. You are kind and in harmony with living, instead of throwing Life around. We have our differences in the human mind and have differing perspectives. However, Awake Living is not attached to our individual perspectives and we are open to the whole, so that human diversity is respected. This receptivity encourages a broader reality for the family, spirituality, society, workplace, environment, science and the arts, so that we live in cooperation, appreciation and acceptance. Since we are Love, we are not searching where to get it. Instead, we are watchful for every opportunity to overflow the greatest gift of the Heart.

Wisdom People

Have you ever gazed into a mirror and noticed that what is looking out has never changed? It is the same awareness that was peering from its cradle beside the bedroom window to see a cherry blossom bobbing in the breeze. It is the same ageless awareness that was watching the clouds in the sky that day on the beach, when you were only twenty. However, when you gaze into a mirror, you also notice that the physical image that is embodying this awareness has been changing throughout your life. When the appearance of the outer shell begins to age, perhaps our attitude is that this is happening before its time. This resistant attitude reflects the bias of our culture as we allow wisdom people to slip out of the mainstream without notice and no longer value them for the Life that they are. Awake Living embraces Life as a stream of continuity, regardless of the forms within which it is appearing or whether it has any form at all.

Wisdom people can tend to Life's children, so that someone is truly present with them, while the physically hardy work or take care of living matters in the home. The children then emulate their superior patience, compassion and light-hearted wisdom. When we honor examined lives, we gain their contemplations and reflections from a broader horizon. We prosper from a greater scope of Life and appreciate its natural passage through form.

Awake Living does not fear the death of form, since we have already realized a mental death. In this death, Consciousness detached from form and we realized the only Life that is. With or without the experience of form, Life itself never changes. Therefore, we welcome the passage of Life's wisdom people, through the Great Liberation. Certainly, we help them resolve their worldly affairs, but there is something deeper here. We could say that we help them prepare for the after-life, but the truth of the matter is we are serving Life after-form. This is the same Life that is living within you now.

Awake Living is responsible for all wisdom people and not just our families. If we are watchful, we often meet them daily. We have our "four roses" in hand and could be offering easy gestures. Awake Living nurtures the embodiment of Pure Consciousness as the One Life that is *Awake Joy*.

Life's Children

All children are Life's children and not the property of the family of origin. We nurture the youth for who they really are, while they are becoming the future stewards of Life on earth. Being fully present with Love's child is the primary ingredient for prosperity. We foster an open mind by being receptive and free of bias. A balanced education includes the sciences, arts, psychology, cross-cultural studies, spirituality, well-being, practical and conscious living, emotional intelligence, daily service and other matters of the human being, the earth and its environment. However, education equally directs the child toward a contemplative life. We point to their inner wisdom and their innate curiosity does the rest. Fun activities are naturally present, but we evenly honor the balance of solitude and silence. When we demonstrate the "four roses" in living, Life's children naturally take their bouquets into the world. In this manner, they become ambassadors for the Heart. The greatest power of the child is its ability to love innocently and we are all the guardians of this universal child.

Chapter Five

True Nature's Garden

The invisible breeze of the late afternoon Trades is starting to rustle the palms. The branches sway in the motionless space that embraces them. The forever blue sky reflects the infinite depth of this unknowable Radiance. From an inaudible stillness, the song of a lace-necked dove announces the imminence of sunset. Neither in this world, nor not of it, the body named mine is walking to the ocean's edge, sensing and functioning, as it does.

The power of the true Ocean's Being is deeply sensed, as the sound of the surf crashes in. Yet, the silence is palpable and profound. Each wave surges forth unto the shore and then retreats to reincarnate, while never surrendering its ocean nature. The pristine sweetness of a tropical spring exudes a single perfume from unknown flowers, underlined by sentient Peace. An expansive gratitude swells in Heart for the beauty of this Garden in Paradise.

These Pacific Northwest feet are finally warm in the white sands, as toes sift to a steadfast foundation. Without forethought or cause, my eyes lift offshore to witness a humpback whale breeching the Mystery. Upon disappearing into the deep, the whale leaps once again out of the cool Blue, displaying magnificent grandeur. It is followed by a dolphin that flies into space, suspends for a moment and then playfully disappears into the Deep. The Grace of this dance continues as we rest in welcoming and wonderment. First a whale, then a dolphin, then a whale, circle again and again through the air, just as inevitably as consciousness dissolves to reemerge. The blow spouts of other whales draw near, as if to inquire into the joy of this sacred dance. Similarly, cars begin stopping along the water's edge as transfixed beings emerge in awe of the ongoing aerial display. As the airborne interchange subsides into the emptiness from which it sprang, minds depart in their cars, perhaps never noticing the brilliance of the Immovable Movement.

The sunset displays the palette of the *true* Artist, as harmonizing colors infuse the horizon and mirror the ethereal onto the wispy clouds overhead. The phenomenal green flame flashes, as the sun seems to submerge into the Ocean. Near a tree without a name, twilight offers just enough light to envision the image of a peacock raising and fanning his tail, as though in mating pride. Seemingly overhead, Venus emerges from the Infinite, as though thankful for the darkness to display its motionless Light. We rise to leave, but intuitively pause. A full moon creeps over the mountain, as it begs remembrance on behalf of the Light of the Sun. We marvel at the middle way of Living Joy and the mystical balance of true Love.

From inner quietude, a voice carrying the imprint of time inquires, "Isn't Venus named after the Goddess of Love?"

"Is that you, Mastermind? Yes, someone told me once that from this first Light in the void of night there shines the Mystery of Love."

Mastermind queries, "Since I have your attention, may I ask another question? Is this Garden in Paradise Real or unreal?"

She smiles, "All I can say is that it radiantly is."

Preparation for Meditative Reading

1. Sit back and relax with your eyes closed. Scan the body for tension. If found, do not try to change it. Just be present and welcome it. If the tension dissipates, continue the scan. If the tension persists, just accept it for now and allow it to be. When you feel totally relaxed, relax a little bit more. Then let go and relax even more.

2. Take a deep breath and follow that breath into the lower abdomen. Without effort, simply be aware of your breathing. Notice that breath is breathing the body. I am not asking you to force, modify or control the breath. Deeply relaxed, I am asking you to notice that it happens by itself. Be aware of how delicate the air feels, as it moves in and out of your nose.

3. Can you sense the energy in your body? Focus first on your hands, then your feet and gradually move throughout the body feeling the inner aliveness. Then, shift your attention to the entire energy field. Allow your body to expand into a "great body," a *huge* body, even larger than a tall building. Sense the aliveness of just being expansive and unbound.

4. With your eyes open and attention inward, are you aware of being aware? Globally aware of your breathing, can you sense the stillness and silence in the joy of being?

Practices and Meditations

In Part II: The Eyewitness, Chapter Two: "Realize that I am," I distinguished practices that reinforce the practitioner in comparison to the true meditation of simply being. These experiments in consciousness are to facilitate the joy of being through direct experience. They also test the primary hypothesis of the illusory "I" and its body idea, as well as an experiment to encounter the true "I." The meditations are not meant for one sitting. Keeping this handbook as your friend, you can return frequently to these pages.

1. Presence Meditation

The length of this meditation does not matter and is designed to remove the idea of the practitioner. You will begin noticing gaps in the mind stream and you begin noticing more spaciousness both within and without. Focus on the gaps between your thoughts, rather than the content of thought. Your earnestness and sincere wish to realize wakefulness here and now are essential.

Please sit with your eyes closed and your spine erect. Without forcing breath, please be present with breathing to notice how gently breath is breathing the body. Simply observe your inner world and be the uninvolved observer of your thoughts, emotions and body. Thoughts come and go. What lies between? Feelings and sensations within your body come and go. What is connecting them? Images come and go. What is not moving? Do you notice that the observer is still, while all else passes through the inner space? Who is this observer?

In the beginning, you will find that you identify and attach regularly to thoughts. When you notice, just bring attention back to itself. Be more intensely alert and fully inhabit the body.

2. Silent Space Meditation

With your eyes open, I would like to draw your attention to the silent space around an object in your room or in nature. Please be still and simply listen to this space for awhile. Now, close your eyes with your spine erect and the body relaxed. Do you hear anything externally? If so, notice that the sound emerges from silence. Follow the sound back into silence. Notice that as you begin listening, you have more awareness of silence. Instead of clutching the emerging sound, relax into being the listening. Be purely the listening, without an object to hear. How does it impact your inner world?

3. Inner Silence Meditation

Shift your attention to listen to your inner silence for awhile. In this meditation, you are shifting attention away from the inner objects of thought, emotion and body toward the silence within your inner body. This requires keen attention, which is instinctive. It is a relaxation and not an effort of tense grasping. The more concentrated the attention, the more inner silence you will notice. If a thought arises and you identify, take a deep breath, relax and be more intensely alert. We are not resisting thought. In a resting manner, we are simply being the silence. How silent is being?

4. Testing the Body Hypothesis

With your eyes closed, can you sense a boundary to your physical body? You may feel the chair that you are sitting in or your feet on the floor. However, where the body is free of touching anything, can you tell where the boundary of the body stops and where the space around it begins?

Still with eyes closed, how far can you expand into this spaciousness that surrounds your body? The experience is not that you are separate from space. You are actually being space. Space is within you and all around you. Is the nature of space within, different than the space without? Is there a boundary between the two? How far can you release into the global space both within and without? Is there spaciousness in being?

If thoughts or sensations arise, just let them move freely through your awareness, without resistance or attachment. Sit in the transparency of objectless attention, just simply being. If you notice contraction around being space, take a deep breath and on the exhale, release into expansiveness without boundary.

5. Movement Meditation

As you become established in being, the experiment directly above can become a movement meditation. Rather than sitting, walking through nature is a good starting point. Then, you move through life's normal activities, while abiding as that same expansiveness with attention to purely being. In movement meditation, forms come and forms go. Office work or home chores appear and then disappear. There is sleeping and then waking. Everything comes and goes, while you remain expansive, receptive and silently being. You will begin noticing more silence and space everywhere, around all appearances, as well as within your inner world. You focus on being, rather than the external or internal appearances. In this meditation, you will realize that your depth of space is unfathomable and that your silence is global and all inclusive.

6. Self-inquiry: Encountering "I"

Please sit with your spine erect and your eyes closed. I would like to draw your attention to your breathing. Without forcing breath, I would like you to inhale deeply and follow the breath into your lower abdomen. On the exhale, sit quietly while being and sharply present with normal breathing. I would like you to hold onto the "I" thought. "I. I. I." If a thought projects outward from "I," such as "I am practicing this exercise," I would like you to draw the thought back inward from where it arose. Follow the sentence backward, word by word, back down the path from where it projected such as, "exercise-this-practicing-am-I." Bring it back to, "I. I. I." Then, I would like you to ask, "Who is practicing?" The answer is, "I am." Not as a mental concept, but the feeling sense of "I am." Then, ask the question, "Who am I?" Listen and rest as silent being. You are drawing the outward bound thought back to "I" and then the outward bound thought "I" back into its Source into the stillness within you. Then, simply rest, "I.I.I." If another thought projects, I would like you to do the same. Such as, "I am reading this book." Follow the path backward, "book-this-reading-am-I." Then ask, "Who is reading this book?" "I am." Looking inward, "Who am I?" Each time, you simply rest as being, while alertly listening. Inquire again with each thought that arises.

The effectiveness should not be underestimated. You can silently inquire at any moment of the day as thoughts arise. The Indian sage, Sri Ramana Maharshi recommended this Self-inquiry to those who could not receive the silent teaching. It can permanently remove identification with the thinker and clearly expose the "I." Self-inquiry tames the outward projecting tendency of thought and turns the mind inward. It then removes the "I" to rest in being within Source. The arising of "I" is the original thought of all other outward bound thoughts. Its pulling power results in the loss of the primal sense of being. Gradually, the length of time that you can rest thought-free will increase, the mind will remain inward and "I" will eventually remain in Source.

7. Devotional Chanting

Robert Gass and On Wings of Song have a seasoned release named *Om Namaha Shivaya*. The original version is a single chant sung over and over for forty-five minutes. It is a beautiful resonation of Grace and I highly recommend it. Allow yourself to be drawn deeply and devotionally into Heart. I ask that you surrender the one who is chanting. Resonate with the chanting. In other words, *be* the chanting. Feel the music move through your body and the energy of Grace flooding your form with a sense of divine devotion. As you chant, you will soon notice that thought is losing momentum as grace and joy come to the forefront.

8. "I am" Meditation

Initially, the Heart space is experienced in your chest. Sit in a comfortable chair with your spine erect, your feet on the floor, your eyes closed and your hands resting in your lap. Take a moment to attend the comfort of the body and let go of any tension to relax more deeply. With each breath, gently inhale the air through your nose and follow it into your lower abdomen. Let the abdomen expand. Continue following the inhaled air as it fills your chest and let your chest expand. On the exhale, keep your attention in the center of your chest as you just let the air go in a relaxed manner, as it leaves your mouth. With attention still in your chest, notice the inner silence at the end of each exhale. Breathing is relaxed and normal.

a. With your head straight forward, inhale and exhale ten times in the manner explained above.

b. Turn your head to the right over your shoulder to inhale. Then, turn your head to your left shoulder to exhale through your mouth. Still looking over your left shoulder, inhale through your nose and then turn your head over your right shoulder again to exhale. Each time, be aware of the silence at the end of each exhale. Repeat this series ten times.

c. With normal, relaxed breathing and your head straight forward, let the silent word "I" fill your chest as you inhale. As you exhale, sense the silent word "AM" in your Heart as you exhale. In the silence at the end of the exhale, sense the silent being in your chest. Repeat ten times.

d. Without the words "I am," repeat the same exercise ten times. At the end, take five minutes to appreciate the aliveness that has flooded your form.

9. Breath Control

Reducing the number of breaths that you take each minute is effective in controlling the thought process. Take longer and slower breaths as you concentrate on each inhale and exhale. Practice each morning and before beginning meditation and you find that the number of thoughts is reduced. Soon, slower breathing will be normal.

10. Breath Retention

You will find that when you are holding your breath, the mind cannot think. Inhale fully in four seconds, hold your breath for eight seconds, exhale in four seconds and then listen to the silence and stillness at the end of the exhale for four seconds. Over time, the normal breathing process will become slower.

11. Life is the Way

In Part IV: The Heart in Chapter Three "Life is the Way" I share the practice of attending the present moment to receive the teachings of the Heart.

12. Four Roses

In Part IV: The Heart in Chapter Four "Awake Living" in the section "Four Roses, " I outline living with compassion, service, gratitude and unconditional Love. This spiritual practice for living our everyday lives is a powerful tool to turn the ego's way into the way of the Heart.

Index of Quotes, Lyrics and References

Contact Katie Davis, Related Websites, Publisher

For information on events by Katie Davis
or to purchase publications:
Katie Davis Website
www.KatieDavis.org

To Schedule an Event or Interview with Katie Davis
contact at awake@katiedavis.org

Related Websites:
Awake Joy Website
www.AwakeJoy.org

Sundance and Katie Website
www.SundanceandKatie.org

Sundance Burke Website
www.SundanceBurke.org

Awake Spirit Publishing is dedicated to publications on awakening, non-duality, the essence of enlightenment and awake living that are in cadence with global transformation, humanity, the living earth, its creatures and environment.

Contact at

Awake Spirit Publishing Website
www.AwakeSpiritPublishing.com

Awake Spirit Publishing, #202
1993 S. Kihei Rd, Suite 21
Kihei, HI 96753 USA

info@AwakeSpiritPublishing.com